GOD'S OWN OFFICE

Praise for the book

'*God's Own Office* is a delightful read. Written with transparent sincerity, James Joseph's story is like an Indian *Walden*, an idyllic going back to Nature without cutting off ties with the everyday corporate world. Joseph's simplicity and unpretentiousness belies the pioneering nature of what he has achieved—a small miracle in today's cut-throat world' —Anil Dharker, writer and columnist, and founder and festival director, Mumbai International Literary Festival

'James has dared to do what most employees and people managers are scared to try. This book is a practical inspiring guide for anyone seeking work-life resonance. A truly refreshing and honest account, a must-read for CEOs and HRD managers trying to unleash the full potential of their employees'—Anil K. Khandelwal, ex-chairman, Bank of Baroda, and author of *Dare to Lead*

'In the age of globalization a professional can work effectively from anywhere in the world, James has proved this very well from his village. *God's Own Office* is the office of the future' —Mohandas Pai, chairman, Manipal Global Education

'In the new economy, there will be fewer and fewer traditional jobs. Companies will rely increasingly on networks of experts who could be anywhere. Far from being scary, this trend creates exciting new opportunities for professionals who have valuable expertise. For this breed, geography is history. Work-life resonance becomes eminently possible. James Joseph shows the way based on the inspiring story of his own journey. Dare to dream!'—Ravi Venkatesan, founder of Social Venture Partners India, and ex-chairman, Microsoft India

GOD'S OWN
OFFICE

HOW ONE MAN WORKED FOR A GLOBAL
GIANT FROM HIS VILLAGE IN KERALA

JAMES JOSEPH

PORTFOLIO
PENGUIN

PORTFOLIO
Published by the Penguin Group
Penguin Books India Pvt. Ltd, 7th Floor, Infinity Tower C, DLF Cyber City,
Gurgaon 122 002, Haryana, India
Penguin Group (USA) Inc., 375 Hudson Street, New York, New York 10014, USA
Penguin Group (Canada), 90 Eglinton Avenue East, Suite 700, Toronto, Ontario,
M4P 2Y3, Canada
Penguin Books Ltd, 80 Strand, London WC2R 0RL, England
Penguin Ireland, 25 St Stephen's Green, Dublin 2, Ireland (a division of
Penguin Books Ltd)
Penguin Group (Australia), 707 Collins Street, Melbourne, Victoria 3008, Australia
Penguin Group (NZ), 67 Apollo Drive, Rosedale, Auckland 0632, New Zealand
Penguin Books (South Africa) (Pty) Ltd, Block D, Rosebank Office Park,
181 Jan Smuts Avenue, Parktown North, Johannesburg 2193, South Africa

Penguin Books Ltd, Registered Offices: 80 Strand, London WC2R 0RL, England

First published in Portfolio by Penguin Books India 2014

Copyright © James Joseph 2014

10 9 8 7 6 5 4 3 2 1

The views and opinions expressed in this book are the author's own and the facts are
as reported by him which have been verified to the extent possible, and the publishers
are not in any way liable for the same.

ISBN 9780670087747

Typeset in Sabon by R. Ajith Kumar, New Delhi
Printed at Thomson Press India Ltd, New Delhi

A PENGUIN RANDOM HOUSE COMPANY

To

My wife, the silver lining of every cloud in my life.
Without her unwavering support and sacrifice,
I couldn't have completed this crazy journey across
three continents.

Our three beautiful daughters, for not complaining
too much about the frequent changes they had
to go through.

My late father, who spent every ounce of his energy
between two accidents to get us through college.

My mother's family for shielding me from her
loss during my early years.

CONTENTS

INTRODUCTION

On 9 October 1974, we had all just returned from church and I suddenly realized something was wrong. I started shouting at everyone around me, 'Ayyo ningalarum ente ammachiye palleennu konduvannilley. POYI AMMACHIYE KOOTTIKONDU VAA. (How come all of you didn't bring my mother back from the church, she is alone there. GO GET MY MOTHER.)' All the villagers grew teary-eyed. I was three years old when my mother died of cancer. Thirty-five years later, I walked on stage at the Philips Arena in Atlanta in front of 14,000 employees from around the world to receive Microsoft's highest award from the CEO, Steve Ballmer. Colleagues from three major continents with whom I had worked at some point in time offered the loudest applause. Many professionals my age have similar success stories to narrate, except that I made the trip to receive the award from the same soil where

I made a whole village cry all those years ago.

The first chapter of this book is a glimpse into the rich contrast of my life in God's Own Office, where I experienced the joy of working for the booming Indian economy while living the well-marinated life of Bharat. The second chapter is about the most common journey of a professional from small-town India to big international cities to become a globally competent professional. The third chapter is about returning home on my own terms without compromising the professional career I painstakingly built over fifteen years. It was only on returning to my village that I felt an absolute work-life resonance. This proved to be the catalyst for starting my journey as an entrepreneur in my backyard. The fourth chapter is a step-by-step guide to plan your own journey to come back home and set up your God's Own Office. The final chapters make a case for companies to embrace this concept.

ONE

WORKING FOR INDIA AND LIVING IN BHARAT

There is equal satisfaction in being a big fish in a big pond and a small fish in a small pond, the former for the professional intellect and the latter for the spirit. There are two experiences which led me to this conclusion.

Several years ago, I was on my way to Chennai to collect my US visa. I boarded the train from Piravom Road, a tiny station in our village, and when the train was about to leave, a six-feet-tall, well-built man boarded the train. He quickly climbed on to the berth above mine and went to sleep without saying hello to anyone in our cabin. He didn't look like a regular second-class train traveller and didn't even fit on the berth. After an hour, he got down, sat with all of us and started chatting with an elderly couple. They were on their way to a school in Orissa, where they had taught for some thirty years, for a function to honour their contribution to the school. As soon as he discovered that they were teachers, he took no time in expressing his appreciation and respect for the teaching profession. He had returned to Kerala with his family after working in Thailand for several years. When he learnt that I had just returned from the UK after acquiring my master's degree and was heading to San Francisco for work, he too shared a little bit more about himself.

His name was Thomas Koshy. He was the president of Thai Carbon Plant owned by the Birla Group until Aditya Vikram Birla passed away two years ago. He and Birla were room-mates at MIT. As soon as Dr Koshy completed his PhD from MIT, Birla asked him to join his business. Once Birla died, Dr Koshy felt it was time to bring his family back to where he had his roots and watch his children grow up in the same place where he had grown up. He said the new chairman, Kumaramangalam Birla, always considered him an uncle and it was more appropriate for the son to build a management team comprising people of his generation.

After returning to Kerala, he started a spice export business and shifted from black carbon to black pepper!

Dr Koshy had an urgent business meeting in Chennai and no flight tickets were available. This was way before private airlines were introduced in India. The only option was to take the second-class train from my station, which had a few reserved seats not known to many people.

It was a Bheem meets Hanuman moment. I was regretting having to travel by second class because of my decision to leave a well-paying job to pursue higher studies in the UK. I had spent all my savings, had no income for almost two years and was heavily in debt. And here was someone who had completed his PhD from one of the best institutes in the world, that too a generation ahead of me. He was the CEO of a big business and a close friend of one of the richest billionaires in the world. He was sitting comfortably in a second-class train next to me. He had moved from being a big fish in a big pond to a small fish in a small pond with relative ease.

My trip to Chennai, during which I met Dr Koshy, was to get my H1 B visa (work visa) stamped and take the next flight to San Francisco to join a lucrative job at the dotcom darling i2 Technologies. But the consulate officer refused to stamp my passport, asking me to return after a month, thereby prolonging my agony. I had to survive another month with the support of my extended family, so I offered my services to anyone who needed an extra hand. When I had nothing else to do, I read or backpacked around the country, exploring India's history and culture.

A month had passed and I was back on the train to Chennai reading *Living with Himalayan Masters* by Swami Rama. I was about to doze off when a tall gentleman dressed in a white robe came to my seat and said, 'Son, can I borrow your book while you are resting? I will return it as soon as you wake up.' He looked like he was in his late seventies. Except a short ponytail, his head was entirely shaved. I lent him the book.

When I woke up, he returned the book and told me that he found it fascinating because it was quite informative about the life and perspectives of an Indian monk. He said it was not normal for a young man like me to find a book like that interesting and asked me more about myself. I wanted to tell him that this book was my only source of strength that was holding me together after enduring the Chinese torture that US immigration and 'neutralization' service was putting me through. Since I'm a salesperson at heart, I decided to give it a positive spin without being untruthful. I told him that I had completed my master's from one of the best universities in the UK, had been living in Las Vegas for the past seven months, and was on my way to Chennai to collect my visa and join a great job in San Francisco.

'Oh, you were living in Las Vegas. I used to visit Vegas twice a year in the seventies, I would go to the Grand Canyon on every trip,' he said, going into a reflective mode. I thought a monk visiting Sin City meant he was part of some kind of cult. He continued, 'I used to work for J.R.D. Tata and was the financial controller for Air India before the government took control of the airline from its founder. I used to visit Vegas for the Boeing conference.' I almost fell off my seat. He was the CFO of one of the largest air carriers in Asia, a crown jewel in aviation at the time. A retired CFO of India's first airline, dressed like a monk and travelling with me on a second-class train, I couldn't resist but ask, 'Sir, what do you do now?' He replied, 'I am the treasurer of Sankarachaya of Kanchi Kamakoti and I also run a foundation to revive the ancient gurukul form of schooling.' He looked absolutely content with what he was doing. Before leaving, he wished me well for my life in the US and asked me to continue my interest in eastern philosophy. Finally, he left me with one quote from a sage: 'Living in another country is like living at your in-law's house, so do come home when you have learned enough'.'

A couple of years ago, I had to organize a CFO Forum for India's top CFOs. It took me almost six months to plan and execute a compelling agenda to convince twenty of them to dedicate three hours of their time for my meeting. During those six months, I'd often think of this monk.

My four years of working for India and living in Bharat kept me oscillating between the big fish and the small fish like a pendulum, my spirit and intellect had finally found their perfect match.

Two snakes between a captain and a governor

One day, I was discussing the agenda for a major leadership event I was organizing for eighty customer executives in Delhi with an external vendor. We were going through the list of speakers they had access to. The speakers that we agreed on included a well-respected retired governor of the Reserve Bank of India and the CEO of one of the largest technology training firms in the country. By this time, I could hear my youngest daughter arguing with my wife in the living room. I predicted a loud scream any moment. So, I walked to my balcony, which gave me two doors of separation from my daughter. The agency suggested a former captain of the Indian cricket team as the star motivational speaker. During this discussion, I looked down from my balcony and saw some unusual movement in the little stream below the apartment. Two snakes coming together and rubbing against each other; I knew exactly what to expect next. I had seen it once about twenty-five years ago. 'James, are you there? I am suggesting the most exciting speaker for the event and you are not showing any enthusiasm, do you have a better speaker in mind?' the vendor said. I replied, 'Anuradha, something urgent and super important has just come up. I will reach out to you over SMS to find another time today to continue this discussion. Sorry to cut you off abruptly, I will explain later. Bye for now.'

I put the phone down, took my DSLR camera and ran out of the flat in my shorts. My wife tried to stop me to find out what was going on, but I had no time to explain. I ran down fifteen floors, clicking pictures from each level. I was afraid the snakes might disappear if I waited for the elevator. I got within fifteen feet of the snakes as they continued their high-energy, romantic and synchronous courtship dance for some time. I sent the pictures with the title 'Snakes in Love' to my company's photography club and they were a huge hit. None of my colleagues knew I did this while balancing work. Taking pictures of the snakes was my version of a coffee break.

A great president who spoiled my Shivaratri

'I gave India the missile as that was needed two decades ago, now India needs the best hackers to be

ahead in the new world of cyber warfare, so I urge you, computer professionals, to produce the best hackers in the world' —Dr A.P.J. Abdul Kalam, former president of India.

One day, I got a call from another agency organizing the annual banking technology awards for the Indian Banks Association (IBA). The date for the awards function needed to be postponed from January to 3 March as requested by the chief guest. The agency wanted to know if I was okay with the date. I told him I would cross check with everyone involved and confirm.

I first checked my calendar and it said: 'Absolutely no travel, if required mark as holiday.' It was Mahashivaratri, a big holiday in Mumbai. More importantly, the largest human gathering in Kerala happens on that night at the Aluva Siva temple, which I can see from my apartment. The temple is situated on the sand banks where the river splits into two and at night on Shivaratri, hundreds of thousands of people gather to pray for their ancestors. The custom is so ancient there is a well-known proverb associated with this huge gathering: *Aluva manppurathu kanda parichayam* (The faintest memory of meeting someone).

I was planning to do a full photo feature on this mega event from my balcony that night, hence the 'no travel' block on my calendar, which I marked the day I moved into our apartment.

I called the agency right away, 'Are you in your right mind to do this event on a holiday in Mumbai? We anyway have a challenge to get bankers for events in Mumbai, why would you even consider it on Mahashivaratri?' They responded, 'James, the IBA board discussed this issue in detail and felt that for this chief guest, bankers will show up on a holiday.' 'And who is this chief guest,' I probed further. 'Dr A.P.J. Abdul Kalam,' the agency said. I thought for a while. Getting the audience was no longer the issue. Where was I going to be, Aluva or Mumbai?

Dr Kalam had left an indelible impression on me over the years. I had read his *Wings of Fire* from cover to cover. Every time I cross the railway bridge over the river to talk to my mentors on our weekly phone call, it brings to mind Dr Kalam's daily walk across the railway bridge as a child in his home town of Dhanushkodi. I had another Bheem meets Hanuman moment with my seventy-year-old barber. To my question on how he kills time between two customers, he pulled out a book neatly wrapped in a newspaper. It was the Malayalam edition of *Wings of Fire*, which he had read four times! The great man's book would help me kill time on a plane and my barber kill time when his customer's chair was empty.

I had no choice but to postpone my Shivaratri photo shoot by a year and go to see the man I had admired for many years.

Don't kill the turtle before meeting Tom Friedman

'Vinod, if you promise you will not kill the turtle until I am back from Mumbai, you can start cleaning the well.' These were my instructions over the phone to my neighbour Vinod just before receiving Tom Friedman in Mumbai for a CFO breakfast meeting.

Back home, I was in the middle of a tough negotiation with Vinod on whether the turtle in my well should become soup for his pregnant wife or whether it should be released into the Periyar river. That morning, Vinod was going to clean my well and take the turtle out. I made a short call to extend the life of the turtle till I was back from Mumbai, and proceeded to the breakfast meeting room with Friedman.

At the meeting, Friedman declared that the 'average is over'. He said that CFOs need to get used to going after the 'cheap genius' who can think like an 'immigrant, an artisan and a waitress'. While he was signing his book, *That Used To Be US,* for me, I explained to Friedman about my journey back home to my village in Kerala and how I had declined lucrative job offers. He patted me on my back and said I belong to the cheap genius group he referred to in his book.

I had great news waiting for me after the meeting; the laws of physics had saved the turtle!

Some months earlier, I had gone to check on the construction work at my small cottage. While inspecting the well on the property, I saw a turtle and a black fish. I had never seen them before as they rarely came up to the surface. When I showed their picture on my mobile, my daughters immediately said, 'Now we have a pet, we can tell our friends, hooray!' I found this to be an easy solution to the promise I couldn't fulfil during our move from the UK. I had agreed to keep a pet in India as I was hoping that we would be staying in an independent house with a garden like in the UK. We ended up living in a flat due to a variety of reasons which I will go into later.

Another day while I was walking to the cottage I spotted a land turtle inside the canal on the way, which looked like the pet turtle I used to own when I was a child. My elder brother, who now lives in the US, led a National Service Scheme camp at a tribal village in Kerala. After they completed building toilets for the villagers, the tribal leader gave him a land turtle as a thank-you gift. The turtle was easy maintenance, would walk around in the house and sometimes scare people because it would just climb over their foot if they were in the way. If he sneaked out of the house, we had a big problem as it was very hard to spot him among the dry leaves in the yard. My brother found a solution; he painted alternate cells on its hard shell white. This made him easy to spot because he looked like a walking chess board. From that point, we never had to worry. Even if he tried to run away, someone in the village would spot him eventually and bring him home.

When it was my turn to go for engineering studies, there was no one left to take care of the turtle. So he was sent to Delhi to a school where my uncle, a Catholic priest, was the principal. He thought the turtle would be a good addition to the small pet zoo in the school. Unfortunately, his gardener thought all turtles live in water and left him in a bucket overnight, only to find him dead the next day. The moment I saw the land turtle in the canal, the sad death of my own pet turtle came to mind. I knew I had to release my well turtle into the river.

I told my daughters that the turtle must be feeling very lonely in the well, so we should release it into the river so that it could find a friend. My second daughter responded saying the turtle is our pet, and I should find another turtle and put that in the well. I showed them the movie, *Free Willy*, in which a boy their age saves a whale from the zoo, and the girls finally agreed. Then I told Vinod to keep the turtle in a bucket of water when he cleaned the well.

I was in for a big surprise. According to Vinod, the turtle belonged to him as he had caught it from the stream nearby a few years ago. He first thought it was a crab and tried to hack it with his knife. You could still see the V-shaped white mark on its shell. Since it was too small, he put it into our well before I bought the property. He believed turtle meat had medicinal value and would be good for his pregnant wife. He was not willing to give it up.

I was not going to get a better chance to redeem the death of our turtle in a bucket in Delhi, or to teach the value of life to my kids. I told Vinod I was willing to buy it from him. I chose not to use more rational arguments, like everything that is on the property legally belongs to me.

As soon as the meeting with Friedman was over, I called Vinod and got some pleasant news. 'Sir, the turtle looked a lot bigger in the water than it actually is. Looks like it didn't get any bigger at all in the last two years and it is too small to cook. So you can have it,' he said. Basic physics, objects appear larger in water than in air! On land, the turtle hid in its shell and shrank to one third the size it appeared in the water. That evening, on my way back from the airport, I swung by my cottage to pick up the little one and we had a 'free turtle' evening at our apartment complex. I let the kids play with the turtle for some time, took some pictures and finally we all marched together, released it into the river and it swam away.

While playing with the turtle, my second daughter

kept saying it had a long nose. My wife and I told her that it was the head which looked like a nose. Later, when I enlarged the image on the computer, I noticed it indeed had a long nose, which my daughter could see as her eyes were much closer to the ground. I looked it up on the Internet and it was a rare pig-nosed soft shell turtle, which can grow up to 20 kg and is on the United Nations' Red List of endangered species. Let's hope no one catches it again and it grows to 20 kg by the time my grandchildren become grandparents.

TWO

GOING GLOBAL

Childhood and first setback

I was the sixth child of my parents, my father worked for the State Bank and my mother was a schoolteacher. Everything was going smoothly, with my dad doing well at work and on a steady career path. After my birth, Dad decided to build a new home closer to the town, hoping that his brother would opt for the family home back in the village. But he ended up owning both houses after the partition and got into a financially tight position. Soon afterwards, my mother fell ill and was subsequently diagnosed with cancer. Doctors operated on her but realized the cancer was too advanced for them to be able to save her. To make things worse, my dad met with a scooter accident on his way back from the hospital and went into a coma with a head injury. Within two years of my birth, we went from being a happy, prosperous family to a being in a dire situation with both my parents at risk. The news of Dad's accident was kept from my mother. Someone would scan the obituary column of the newspaper before it reached her as people were afraid he could die any time. Luckily, my dad survived and regained consciousness after three months, but with a permanent medical condition that restricted him from taking significant responsibilities at work. He sent all his children to boarding schools. Within a year, my mother passed away. All six of us survived this catastrophic event because Dad spent every ounce of his energy and income to ensure we got a good education. My mother's family gave us emotional support and took care of us during the holidays and sometimes even full academic years at their place. Right from my childhood, Dad would reassure all of us by saying, 'I will only retire after my youngest son completes college, so as long as you all study well, I will be able to support your education. After that, you are on your own.' The reassurance from my mother's family was, 'Your mother is sitting very close to god and if you remain good and do well in academics, she will secure a springboard for you to jump higher than others.' So, I was constantly reminded by everyone around me that my survival of this catastrophic event solely depended on how much knowledge I am able to acquire. I call it my 'Bha-rati mantra'—*rati* for *bha* means lust for knowledge.

First springboard

My boarding-school years were fairly event free, except that I was good at chess and it was always a challenge to tell my friends where my home was. Dad's job required compulsory transfer every three years and changing rental homes frequently was a norm. Sometimes I wouldn't have a clue where our new home was until I visited the place during my next vacation. My first springboard came right after the twelfth standard; I surpassed all my peers at school at the engineering state entrance test. The news spread quickly through the village. At the time, we were staying at my dad's family home so that we could all complete our eleventh- and twelfth-standard studies at the local college. Dad would come home only during weekends and the responsibility of running the house was passed on to the one joining college each year. Since I was the youngest, I had to lock the house again when I left for engineering.

Second setback

Engineering college was a lot of fun. Clearing the entrance was a big boost to my confidence and with this extra confidence, I started getting involved in students' union activities. I still managed to clear all my tests with above average marks, but not up to my earlier standards at school. Just before final year, we decided to float a new party and take on the challenge to win our final year elections. We won the elections, but I lost one paper because of the distraction, which was not a big deal as I could easily clear that before the finals. By this time, Dad had retired and moved to Delhi to be with my eldest brother, who was the only one who had settled down with family. A couple of months before my exam, Dad sent a cheque of an amount much larger than the monthly cheque he used to send. In the accompanying letter, he wrote, 'I trust you in managing your money and hence sending the whole amount you need to finish your studies. I hope you will be able to find a job before you require more money.' That was his last letter to me. During my final exams, I got a call from my brother saying he had been in a minor bike accident and Dad, who was riding pillion, had injured his head during the fall and was still unconscious. He urged me to complete my exams before coming to see Dad. When I arrived in Delhi, he was still in a coma. Within a week, he started showing some signs of recovery and, as suggested by the doctors, we brought him home and provided round-the-clock nursing care. After spending some more days with him, I came back to write my last paper. Unfortunately, Dad passed away the day after I returned. The timing of his death from another scooter accident after eighteen years seemed as if he had been given a lease of life only to provide all six of us basic education so we could stand on our own. Though I returned from Delhi to take the test, I could not pass and lost six months. This was my first academic failure.

Second and third springboards

After six months, I cleared the paper and went to Delhi to look for a job. While many of my friends who graduated earlier than me were still looking for a placement, I was selected to work at an auto component factory called Minda Industries. I got the job through a reference from my uncle, the school principal who had taken in my pet turtle. My confidence was very low, I couldn't speak Hindi or English well. I wasn't even sure if I would be able to perform like an average engineer as I could not even pass in my first attempt. But I worked hard and, within six months, made a good impact at the factory, from the level of assembly line workers to the management. I was in charge of quality and, with great support from my first manager, within eighteen months we reached zero-defect status and displaced the competition at our number one client. Everything was going well—I had regained my lost confidence.

Then came my next springboard. My brother's brother-in-law who used to work for 3M in Minnesota was on a business visit to India and suggested that I apply for a vacant position at 3M India. I applied and I was invited to interview for a sales job. The interview process was smooth and I got selected without any trouble, though real trouble was waiting for me. After a great farewell party at Minda, I joined work at 3M's Delhi office. After the initial round of introductions, I realized I had joined a completely different league of people than the one I was used to working with in the factory. These were the well-dressed, smooth-talking IIT+IIM gang and I was sitting there with my broken English, unable to even wear a tie properly. I was a real misfit and had made a big mistake by leaving my comfortable factory job, even though that had paid much less.

To avoid embarrassment, I spoke little in office, immersed myself in product literature and would jump out to meet clients as often as possible. My clients were mostly automobile factories in and around Delhi and I felt a lot more comfortable being in those factories than in office. Whenever I had free time at the client's site, I would hang out with the engineers on the shop floor. Watching cars being assembled, robotic welding machines, hearing the sound of heavy metallic presses and the beautiful colours of cars coming out of the paint shop was a lot more fascinating than watching my colleague's in office practise the art of negotiation and close deals. They would be speaking on two or three phones at the same time while my phone hardly ever rang. While my colleagues spent all their time offering discounts and chasing collections, I kept my sole focus on figuring out an idea to increase the amount of 3M tape—the product I was supposed to sell—in the most popular car at that time. I earned the trust of a small customer, Polyplastics, based in a town in the neighbouring state of Haryana by advising them on how to improve quality and productivity in their factory. I never had to discuss orders or payment terms with them as they preferred to use my time for help with their factory.

Later, I suggested to Polyplastics that they get into a new product and introduced them to one of 3M's customers in Japan. Within three months, they signed a joint venture with the Japanese firm. The new product increased the consumption of 3M tape from six inches to 3.6 metres. My sales went through the roof, way beyond what one could forecast at the beginning of the year. My salary and bonus all started looking up, but most importantly, I got accepted by a league in office I thought I would never be able to fit into.

The going-global bug

When everything was going well at 3M, I stumbled on an article in the *Times of India*'s *Ascent*. It was called

How to Become a Global Manager and it went on
to explain that a global manager was someone who
could manage a global business from anywhere in
the world. This was the time when the then finance
minister Manmohan Singh was opening up India's
economy and many MNCs were entering the country.
At the same time, demand for Indian talent abroad
was also going up as the baby boom generation started
retiring. The article listed the requirements clearly:
Internationally recognized degree and multinational
company experience across three large markets in the
world. I only had one MNC experience in one large
market and my engineering degree didn't qualify as
an internationally recognized one. I had attempted
the IIM entrance twice and I knew I had no chance.
The British Council in Delhi was having an expo of
UK universities and I eventually got admission at
the Warwick Manufacturing Group at University of
Warwick without a scholarship. Two factors helped
me take the plunge. First, both my parents had passed
away and I was single, so only I needed to face the
consequences of my decision. Second, my boss, Shashi,
an IIM-A graduate, encouraged me to go even though
my leaving would create a void in his team. Till then,

I was just going with the flow and waiting for a springboard to take me to the next level. Now, for the first time, I was taking control of my journey. I left for the UK with every penny I had and a huge loan from my brothers.

The global journey

Warwick was a great start for my global quest. Almost 95 per cent of my classmates were international students. I had a map of the world in my room to look up the country every time I met someone new. The campus flat I stayed in had eight students from five countries. I had a great time at Warwick and made a lot of friends from around the world. During induction, everyone said they chose Warwick for its international reputation and high ranking, but I disappointed a few lecturers when I said I was there because I failed to get into an IIM even after two attempts. Students are treated as paying customers and I would sit in the front, actively debating with the lecturers how I could apply their theories either in the factory where I worked or at 3M. One big plus point at Warwick was that my broken English was still better than the English spoken by some of the international students, and I ended up presenting all group projects. Within a few months I overcame my chronic stage fright. I realized the value of money for the first time in my life; I would think three or four times before buying a soft drink. From a well-respected job at 3M, I switched to washing dishes at the campus canteen to make an extra buck so I could attend the campus parties. Every time I was close to securing a scholarship, it would slip out of my hands at the last minute. Same was the case with job interviews in the UK. This was the last year of the Conservative Party before Tony Blair got the Labour Party to power, and the economy was at its lowest point in the UK. One day, Blair landed in a helicopter on the ground in front of my room and came to our department to declare that with Warwick Manufacturing Group, he would revive UK's manufacturing. By that time, anyone with remote experience in manufacturing in the UK had the title of 'international consultant'. I don't think anything ever changed for UK manufacturing even after a decade of economic growth once Blair came to power, but the service sector thrived. My lucky break was that 3M UK sponsored my thesis project as Shashi wrote to them to help me. That covered all my travel expenses and

I had a real-life international logistics model to study between 3M and Ford, which came in handy later.

Third setback, and a big one

My plan was to get a job abroad after my studies, pay off the huge debt, get international experience and then return to India with a plum post. But I returned empty-handed from Warwick, completely broke and with no job. My brother, who was based in the US, suggested that I visit him for my niece's baptism before I started work. Right after the baptism, I went to a job fair in San Francisco where two companies expressed interest in talking to me further. They were the top two names in supply chain management software. When I did some research on supply chain management, I realized it was the new buzzword for logistics, which was my thesis project at Warwick. Within days, I got a plum offer from the number one firm, i2 technologies, to be based in the beautiful city of San Francisco. 3M was one of their earliest customers and my supply chain thesis and past experience with 3M came in handy. The offer was so good that I could pay off my debt in months. I went from zero to hero! i2's immigration lawyers suggested that I change my visitor's visa to a work visa, and the process was started right away. A week before I was to get my visa, the quota for the H1-visa cap was reached. i2's lawyers asked me not to worry as there was a fair share of lobbying going on to increase the visa cap. Just then, there was a shootout at Capitol Hill, the Senate was shut down immediately and the bill couldn't be placed before recess, which was for a few months. I had no choice but to return to India and wait for the quota to reopen.

Back in India, I went to Chennai for the visa interview. When my turn came, they gave me another shocker: 'Mr Joseph, we need more time to review your papers. Please come back after a month.' I returned to the US consulate after a month and got another shocker: 'Mr Joseph, we are not happy with your papers. We need to send them for further investigation and we can't tell you how long it will take.'

I was completely disheartened. I had now been out of a job for more than two years with a huge debt that would take forever to pay off if I worked in India. I wondered if this was punishment for giving up a solid job at 3M over a stupid newspaper article. My cousin arranged a meeting with a recruiter in Chennai and within a month, I got a semi-decent job at Ford in Chennai, though definitely not on a par with the level I would have been at had I just stayed with 3M in Delhi. I bit my ego and started working for Ford. Unlike 3M, Ford was just entering India. Every morning, I would start at 6 a.m. and walk half a kilometre. The bus would pick us up at 6.15 a.m. I would sleep on the bus till I reached the plant at 7.15 a.m. The day would start with a very spicy breakfast at the canteen, which was torture for my stomach since I had got used to bland food over the past two years. I put my head down and worked. We had a great set of youngsters in the team and a lot of expats from the US and Europe helping us set up the new operation. One good thing about Warwick was that I had become more comfortable working with people from all nationalities and genders. Everyone appreciated that I could represent the firm well, especially with the international delegates of our clients. Moreover, I still had a lot of goodwill with the clients I used to manage at 3M.

Finding my pearl from the gutter

Almost a year passed at Ford without any major

incidents or breakthroughs for me, except for a few overseas trips to represent the Indian team. I received a call from my brother based in Kerala. He said that he had met a medical student from Vienna, who was in Kerala for a month-long internship at a hospital. The student's family wanted to meet me to discuss marriage. After a two-year break from work, I had no appetite to look for a job in another country, that too a non-English speaking one. I told him that I had no interest in going to Vienna, so there was no point in seeing her. He said that she was willing to move back to India. That got me really curious. We met and we liked each other. She convinced me that she was genuinely interested in coming back to India as she felt there were more people in need of doctors in India than in Vienna.

From that point, everything was on the fast track, just like a dream. We met a couple of times and she went back to Vienna with the hope that we would remain in touch. We decided we would get married after she completed her studies in Vienna, which would take about fifteen months. A week after she left, I got a call from the US consulate, saying, 'We couldn't find any fault in your application and if you could kindly send your passport, we will issue the visa.' I thought to myself: 'What's the point in getting the visa eighteen months after a job offer?' As a polite gesture, I called i2 in the US. My hiring manager had been transferred to Europe six months earlier and I was connected to HR. They said, 'Your offer is still valid, we were chasing your case all this time, we want you to join us as soon as possible.' Later, I realized that they had created an email ID for me within the company and marked a copy to that ID on all developments related to my visa. Since I hadn't joined them, I never received those emails.

After discussing this with my fiancée, I resigned from Ford and took the next flight to the US via Vienna. When she finished her studies, we travelled to India, got engaged at her family church and got married at my family church.

Life in the US

I had rocky start at i2. Since my hiring manager had moved to Europe, they put me under the next best logical team in San Francisco. i2 was growing so fast that nobody had time to sit down and discuss anything. My new boss was really busy; his secretary found me a place to sit and told me that she would arrange for my tickets to fly to Dallas, i2's headquarters, to attend the next boot camp. I was curious. 'What is a boot camp?' I asked. She said that it was a type of employee orientation.

The next day, some fifty of us from across the US started our boot camp. It was nothing like the employee orientation I had attended at 3M or Ford. It was rapid-fire training on how to implement i2 software applications on customer sites. We had a tough trainer who kept on reminding us that there would be a test at the end of the two-week training and the results would be sent to our boss, the boss's boss and their boss. Two days into the training, I was completely lost. I had no idea what I got myself into and I had no confidence of passing this nonsensical training. I realized what had happened. They hired me as a supply chain consultant to analyze customers' supply chain, like I did for 3M. However, that organization had been completely changed since, hence they put me into the software implementation team because anyone from India is a techie anyway!

I managed to get ten minutes on the phone with my boss. He asked me to hang in there and complete the training without worrying about the test results. He said that though the training may look overwhelming, it was the best way to understand the company and its products, which would help when I analysed customer supply chains. I tried to make the best of the boot camp, made a lot of good friends. A majority of people at the boot camp were from India, mostly hired from IIM or IIT campuses with a master's degree from one of the Ivy League schools in the US. There were also several people from the US with substantial experience, including one from the US Navy with more than twenty-five years' experience in logistics. Another, a world class surfer, only worked between surfing seasons. From freshers to veterans, everybody was talking about i2 stocks, stock options, stock purchase plans, etc. While I was breaking my head to figure out how to install Gregorian calendar and build a multi-layer forecasting model, someone would shout, 'Our stock just went up by twenty dollars, I wish we would get bought out by someone soon, all our stocks will vest and I won't need to work anymore.' Eighteen months earlier, when I was negotiating my salary, I didn't know anything about stock options and nothing was mentioned in my offer letter.

After three gruelling weeks, I somehow survived the boot camp, got back to the Bay Area in San Francisco and met my boss, Ben, to sort out my posting. 'James, I need to be brutally honest with you. When you were hired, there was one team across all verticals to analyse customer supply chains. Since we have grown so much, that team has been broken into each industry vertical, the experience requirements have changed and there are no positions open in the automotive vertical. Good news is that you are part of the largest vertical, the semiconductor industry, and we can give you more training and time to get you up to speed. Don't worry, software implementation is not that tough, we all learned it on the job,' Ben said. I wasn't too happy, but I had to agree as I needed to pay my loans. Then I inquired if I was supposed to get any stock options, which everyone else at the boot camp got. 'Everybody gets stock options, I will check it out for you and get back to you,' he said as he got back to his email and I returned to my desk. A few minutes later, he stopped at my desk and gave me a book titled *Unix for Dummies* and said I would be put on a project with Sun Micro Electronics. I needed to go to Atlanta for another training before I started work. Ben gave me a post-it note with a number scribbled on it and whispered, 'That's your stock option while joining. I feel it is low as it was set eighteen months ago and I will get you more every quarter to make up for it.'

I set aside the book and got on the Internet to check the value of i2 stocks to multiply it with the number he gave me. A whopping fifteen times the amount I spent at Warwick—if I could just hold on to my chair for four years or if someone bought i2—that's what I would get over and above my salary! I thought an eighteen-month wait was definitely worth it, but my happiness soon turned into anger against two idiots when I checked the stock price eighteen months earlier. I was a pre-IPO hire and the stock had split twice. The first idiot was the one who shot the security guard in Capitol Hill and the second was the one who, sitting at the US consulate in Chennai, not only ripped me off eighteen months of Bay Area salary, but a huge fortune in i2 stocks as well. My phone rang just then. It was my fiancée from Vienna and I was quickly reminded that had it not been for those two idiots, I would never have met her!

I soon went for my written test so that I could get permission to take driving lessons. After clearing the test, the officer asked me if I had a licence from another state. I mentioned I had one from the 'state of Kerala', which he thought was another state in the US, and issued me a full licence! After the training in Atlanta, I spent the next six months working on the Sun project at the i2 headquarters in Dallas.

At the consulting project, I felt like a dummy as I had never worked on computer programs. I even wrote to my friends from Warwick that my life was stuck between the forward slash and backward slash in a Unix box. I was about to complete the project after resolving most bugs through the product team when Sun decided to cancel the project and I could make a graceful exit. Ben then allowed me to go on a consulting assignment to analyse the supply chain of a major van lines for the product I was working on. An exciting engagement at Fort Wayne, Indiana, and I had a critical role in landing a multimillion-dollar deal by making one of the business heads admit that his division would double its growth if they could get what we presented to them. Everybody was pleased and Partha from the product team asked me to join them as their business development head.

My fiancée and I had our wedding in India, honeymoon in Maldives, one reception in Vienna and another at my brother's place in Las Vegas. Finally, we got back to Dallas and started our life together. As soon as my wife started preparing for her exams for medical specialization in the US, our first child announced her arrival.

Everything was going well during the Clinton era as economic growth continued. Then came a series of shocks: the dotcom bubble burst, Enron went belly up and more bad news followed for the economy. One day, my wife asked me, 'What is Down Jones? And why do they keep saying it's going down?' That summed up the overall mood. Just before my stock options were to vest, i2's stock came crashing down and went under water, which meant the market price was lower than the price at which they awarded my stock options at the time of joining. I didn't get a single penny of the money I once dreamt of.

One day, I was driving to work when my wife called to say a plane had hit one of the buildings in New York. Everybody from our team was gathered in the TV room and we watched as another plane crashed into the second tower. Two buildings in flames with people jumping off. When the buildings collapsed, we decided to go home. We called everyone we knew to make sure they were all safe. After 9/11, the dotcom bust accelerated and over the next nine months, there were three layoffs during which our team went from sixty to six. I was under threat twice at a time when my wife was pregnant but luckily survived. Right after our first daughter was born, Partha connected me with a partner of i2 in the Bay Area called Informatica. I managed to find a job with them as a supply chain product marketing manager.

My initial days at Informatica involved hectic travel across the US for product road shows, analyst tours, conferences, etc. We had a great team and my marketing campaigns were impactful. Analysts took a special liking for me as I had real-life manufacturing industry experience with 3M and Ford. However, the economic stimulus introduced by the President made no impact except that I got a $600 check from the government for the first time. The country had already moved away from the Alan Greenspan era of irrational exuberance of economic confidence to the Donald Rumsfeld era of irrational exuberance of military confidence. So, our marketing campaigns only had limited influence and things started slowing down at Informatica as well.

I was given the additional responsibility of managing

all product pricing, which made my role global as any sales person anywhere in the world required my intervention to make an exception in the price of any product. The flipside was that I couldn't take leave in the month-end, quarter-end or year-end periods. I had to get online within an hour of getting a call to review and approve any exception so the deal could be processed. If I was late, the deal could slip to the next month, quarter or year. However, I was only required to work if I got a call and the maximum I needed to spend was one hour in the morning and one hour in the evening. Most people took time off during the year-end and I would be alone in the office. I came up with a solution and this was my first experiment with remote working efficiently. We would go on drive tours along the West Coast during that time and I would map a route in such a way that at any point I could reach a location with an Internet connection within an hour. It worked perfectly and I ended up getting more holidays than others.

Later, my brother and family visited us from Las Vegas for a long weekend and it was my turn to take him to a good golf course. He had taken me to some of the finest golf courses in Las Vegas and we both really enjoy playing golf as that gave us time to chat about everything from family back home to work and future plans. This time, I took him to Halfmoon Bay Golf Links near the Bay Area overlooking the Pacific Coast. It was a very foggy morning and there was no way we could see the greens or the yard markings. We decided not to worry about our score and instead focused on enjoying the beautiful location and chatting. One of the topics we discussed was returning to India. My brother told me that it was no longer an option for him as the combined hold of his children's roots in America was stronger than his own hold in India. A childhood memory of a leech walking on the ground came to my mind. Similar to inchworms (caterpillars of geometer moths), they walk measuring the geometer of earth one inch at a time. First, they stand on their rear legs, arch forward an inch and once the front legs establish grip, they drag the whole body towards the front. I suddenly realized that if my wife studied for her specialization in the US and waited a few more years to gain experience, I would be in the same boat as my brother. The possibility of returning to India would be a closed chapter. I had to make a decision. Should I continue to enjoy our professional growth in the US and settle down for good or could we change course and return to India without losing out on professional growth?

THREE

RETURNING HOME

I wasn't ready to return to India yet as I hadn't completed one requirement from the newspaper article. I had an international degree, good work experience at MNCs in Asia and North America and had worked in global roles. However, I was missing one more market. Even though I had studied in the UK, I had no work experience in Europe. I told my wife, 'Why go through the pain of specializing in the US if we are not going to settle down here? If we go to Europe, you can start a practice straight away without any certification.' I suggested that we try in the UK first, where I could also work. She was thrilled and agreed instantly. I was tired of working for companies like i2 and Informatica, which were smaller as compared to 3M or Ford. The quarterly pressure on such companies from Wall Street was too great and any long-term strategy at best had a three-month life. I usually need six months to immerse myself into a large problem, come up with an out-of-the-box strategy and stay on course till I turn things around. I realized that I had to work for a 3M equivalent in the software industry, which would help me with my final move to India. Microsoft was the only company that fit the bill. I took a printout of the Microsoft UK campus in Reading and kept it at my desk. I also asked my wife to look for a job at the Royal Berkshire Hospital next to the Microsoft campus. She managed to land an interview there.

Fortunately, my wife got the job. I told my boss, Sanjay, about my desire to get work experience in Europe and he agreed to discuss it with the European team and help me out. In the meantime, my wife and I travelled all over America to experience its beauty before leaving for the UK.

By the first week of January, there was still no firm decision on my transfer to Europe. I knew I had to do something to force a decision. I informed Sanjay that my wife had got a job in the UK already and with or without a transfer, I had to move by end of the month. That made it easy for Sanjay as he could position it as a move to retain a good employee. Within a week, I had the approval to join as the European product marketing manager based out of the UK.

I started work. Half of us from the European marketing team were based in the UK and the other half were spread across Europe, responsible for respective country marketing. Our boss spent each day of the week in a different country, which meant he managed us from an aeroplane. I created an alert on the Microsoft UK career site so that I got an email notification whenever a role which suited my profile opened up.

The Informatica UK office was tucked away in the beautiful countryside near Maidenhead called White Waltham. Apart from our office building, there was a warehouse, several pubs and an airfield that was used during World War II. Monday to Thursday, we would all queue up at the only sandwich counter inside the warehouse yard. I would have an Italian tuna panini, the only option if you wanted something warm and slightly spicy.

On my first Friday at the office, a colleague came over to my desk and said, 'James, on Fridays we all go for a pub lunch. Would you like to join us?' I didn't know what a pub lunch was. But anything would taste better than the fifth Italian tuna panini of the week, so I agreed. The custom was that they would pick a new pub each week, even if it was a bit of a drive, and have a good two-hour social outing. The first question I was asked when I arrived at the pub after a twenty-minute drive through small roads between farms and a period church took me by surprise: 'James, what would you like to drink, a beer or some wine?' I had never refused a drink when I had gone out with office colleagues before, but nobody had ever offered one during lunch break, after which I was supposed to go back to work. The workshop where we used to practice at our engineering college had a big sign: 'Work is worship; treat this place like your place of worship.' Here I was, posed with a question that could mean getting back to my place of worship drunk. I came up with a clever response to decline the offer: 'I have to drive back, so I will pass.' They promptly responded, 'We will be here for two hours and based on your weight, you can have a pint of beer or a glass of wine and you will still be within the permissible limit to drive.' I ended up having a pint of Guinness and some fish and chips. We had a great time and I enjoyed the concept as it was a great way to bond with my office colleagues. They later told me that they suspected I was a mole imported by the headquarters to spy on the European operations! I didn't want to tell them that my remote control was an article in an Indian newspaper, which even the author may not have given serious thought to.

After I started studying the European business, I realized that there was a genuine problem. All the material they were getting from the headquarters had US customer stories and none from European countries, except a few from the UK. European customers claim that their situations are different than the US and do not give much credit to US stories. There were several stories in each country, but only in their respective languages. My first victory was coming up with a cheat-sheet with European customer stories by translating all local language stories to English and converting the consolidated stories from Europe back to the respective countries.

On the personal front, we continued our road trips

in the UK and soon realized that it was cheaper and more exciting to spend our vacations in Europe than in the UK, even if that meant taking a flight. Every six months, we would visit my wife's family in Vienna and also explored places such as Italy, France, Germany and Hungary whenever we got a chance. Life went along smoothly and just before the arrival of our second daughter, we bought our first house in the UK. I made sure it was within a couple of miles from the Microsoft UK campus, even though I still had no luck getting an interview call despite applying for several roles over one year.

Six months after we moved into the new house, I got my first interview call at Microsoft for a fairly junior role given my profile. The hiring manager, Steve, went through my résumé and, after a few discussions, said, 'This role will not even tickle your brain, so I can't hire you. But seeing your postcode, we can't let you go. I will speak to a few people and we will find a role for you.' Within a month, I started working for Microsoft as the industry marketing manager for the manufacturing sector.

Origins of working from home

Life at Microsoft was very similar to life at 3M. I had an excellent manager, John, who understood that with my wife working nights and weekends, I could only travel abroad four times a year with advance notice. He usually worked from home on Fridays. One Friday, he came to office for a meeting and found me working all alone. He asked me why I was working from office on a Friday and I retorted, 'Why do you all work from home on Fridays?' Then he patiently explained that most people lived in London and Friday evening traffic to London was horrendous. If people worked from home on Friday, they could enjoy the weekend with their family as soon as they finished work. They didn't have to waste another two hours stuck in traffic. Then he asked me to check out his and other managers' Friday calendars. I noticed a lot of conference calls on Friday, while all physical meetings were scheduled for the rest of the week.

Even though I had a very short commute to office, it was too boring to go on Fridays. So I converted the smallest bedroom in our house, which overlooked the back garden, into my home office. I started working from there on Fridays. I could watch squirrels, birds and my kids playing in the garden while I worked. Before it got dark, I would take them to the park nearby.

Mastering the art of experiential engagement

At Microsoft, I started experimenting with customer roundtables where we got together a small group of customers and subject matter experts on a topic relevant to Microsoft. I soon realized that a happy customer can articulate the benefits of the solution better than the best sales person at Microsoft, and customers won't even charge you to speak. So I used the budget usually marked for a speaker's fee to include a unique experience for the meeting. While most people held their meetings at conference rooms in hotels, I looked for unique venues like a customer location, a box in Wembley stadium along with a tour to the dressing room of English football superstars, or a palatial multimillion-pound penthouse which senior executives would like to own before retirement. In addition, I started booking the top tables at prestigious industry awards and black-tie dinners in the UK for my customers. With the help of my mentor, Peter, I progressed from being the organizer to the main host of these meetings. My meetings were attended by our best customers and I always received excellent feedback.

One of my colleagues at Microsoft UK, Manoj, was also from India and had a similar background. During my second week there, he asked me about my long-term plans and told him that I wanted to move back to India in three to five years. He dismissed it right away and said that's what every Indian professional says at the beginning. He asked me the question once every year and in the third year, he said, 'You have been saying three to five years. You are already in your third year; I don't think you are serious.' Then I got a message from Jon, the head of an industry vertical from the US who used to fly down for one of the black-tie dinner awards I used to sponsor every year. He said that a senior person called Michael from HQ, working on special projects in the energy sector, was visiting the UK and asked if I could join his meeting. I looked at the profile and realized that Michael used to head our Asia-Pacific business before he moved back to HQ. After the meeting, I asked him whether he had a taxi back to London. Michael said that he was very conscious of his carbon footprint, and would take public transport to the train station and the train back to London. I grabbed the opportunity and told him that the train station was on my way home and, if it was okay with him, I could drop him. He agreed. During those twenty minutes, I expressed my desire to move back to India and contribute to my country. Things moved really fast from there and within six months, Manoj and our family friends were hosting a farewell party for us! Manoj still felt that we would come back after six months, so he asked me to hold on to the house till we were really sure.

Michael sent a mail to Ravi Venkatesan, the then chairman of Microsoft India. Ravi reached out to me asking about the roles I was interested in. I had several options: a smaller role in my home town in Kerala to working on a strategy role in the chairman's office or the same role I had in the UK. Michael preferred the role in the chairman's office. My mentor, Peter, knew of my desire to move to my home town and suggested that I choose the smaller role directly instead of moving my family again one more time. But after moving from the US to the UK, I realized it is much harder to move as a family, and it was better to reduce the number of variables. So, I opted for the same role I held in the UK, which helped me hit the ground running at work and free up time to help my family settle down in India. My wife was seven months pregnant. I also had to do some tough negotiations to allow me to work from Bangalore rather than the India head office near New Delhi. This was part of my strategy to get people used to working with me without seeing me, for my eventual plan was to move back to my home town. In any case, Kerala was the only option because Malayalam was the only Indian language that my wife spoke. As a doctor, it was a prerequisite that she converse in the local language.

In the first few months, I visited all the offices and took stock of the situation, and within three months, I had a plan. By this time, our third daughter arrived, which made our family truly global. Three girls born on three different continents and I had completed all requirements mentioned in that newspaper article. During the ten years I spent abroad, India had experienced terrific economic growth and many companies from India had become global companies. Many of my friends who stayed back in India rode the wave and were now at very high positions in various companies. The question was whether my global learning would help me perform in India or whether it was going to be irrelevant. I may even have lost the knack of working in India.

Three months after I landed in India, I started using the customer speaker-led experiential engagement model I mastered in the UK in partnership with the sales team. We hit bullseye from the first one in Chennai and went on to replicate the model successfully across all major cities. Whatever I used to do in one city in London, I had to do in five cities in India, which meant I only spent a fifth of my time in the Bangalore office. On Fridays, I used to work from home like in the UK. During the holidays, we would drive down to our home town in Kerala and scout for good locations where we could settle down. I invested in a property ten minutes from the Kochi airport and within a 45-minute drive to my ancestral home. I continued with this hectic schedule for a year, got an excellent review and decided it was time for me to make the next move.

Final push to come home

Bangalore airport was shifted to a location outside the city. It took an hour-and-a-half to get to the airport from the city and another forty-five minutes to check in. I said to my manager, Punit, 'Considering the amount I travel, I will be better off living closer to the airport in Kochi than in Bangalore, and my wife will also be able to get back to work.' Punit was open to the idea, but it required further approval. He came back with a negative response and I waited for another opportunity.

During my next career-development discussion with my skip-level manager (immediate manager's manager), Tarun, I again brought up the topic of moving to my home town. While talking about my future plans, I told him that my stay in India was quite uncertain. I explained that it was important for me to move to Kerala where my wife could work, or I would have to return to the UK as soon as I completed my three years in India. I made my final plea: 'If you allow us to move, we are here for good.' That convinced Tarun and he came back with conditional approval. 'We are making an exception for you because we know your work ethic. But we will watch your performance for six months and if it goes down, you are coming back,' he said. I had finally got it! We secured admission for our kids at a school near the property we had bought, which was still under construction, and moved to Kerala within three months.

At my home office, I would start work at 6 a.m. with my cup of tea and would complete half the day's job by the time most of my colleagues reached office after a long commute. I continued with my signature experiential customer engagement. I took the model to international locations by hosting meetings on the top floor of the Burj Al Arab, the Petronas Towers and a spectacular location in Phi Phi Island—all at a lower cost than hosting such meetings in India. I enjoyed the contrast between my work and home life—one morning I was bumping into Steve Ballmer at a gym in Hyderabad, the next morning I was collecting a fresh catch of prawns from the backwaters of Kochi with my daughter. Another day, I was speaking to a group of executives from the leading public sector enterprises about global engineering skills shortage and the next day, I was speaking to a group of farmers at an island near my home about the benefits of inviting professionals to participate in their farm.

The Oscar comes home

Six months passed and about the time my performance was to be reviewed, my phone rang at 6 a.m. It was a text message from, Tarun, my skip-level manager: 'Check email and take a bow!' There was an announcement from the Microsoft India chairman, Ravi Venkatesan, saying that I had won the Circle of Excellence award, the highest award at the company. The benefits included travelling to the US to collect the award from Steve Ballmer at our sales conference and attending a dinner with the top leadership. That year, Microsoft was rated as the best employer in the world. Here I was, after completing all the requirements of that newspaper article, receiving one of the best employee awards from the best employer in the world. I was in a small village working out of what I called God's Own Office. I just needed to find a product to manage a global market from here.

I went on to work out of God's Own Office for another three years and it remained my own little secret till I spoke about it at a Confederation of Indian Industries (CII) conference in Kochi. Kris Gopalakrishnan, then CEO of Infosys and president of CII South, suggested that I document and share my experience so that more professionals could return to their home towns. Five years after returning to India, with a heavy heart, I decided to leave Microsoft and, more importantly, the executive engagement role I considered tailor-made for me. The timing was right as my wife was about to get her licence to practice and the time I took to write the book would allow her to re-establish herself in her profession. I intended to get back to the professional world to do a global role from my God's Own Office, but god had a different plan and I accidentally discovered my calling to promote a humble fruit from my backyard.

JackFruit365™ My start-up for a social cause

'Serendipity is looking for a needle in a haystack and finding the farmer's daughter,' said the late Roger Needham, who set up Microsoft's first overseas research centre in Cambridge, UK, quoting Sir Hans Kornberg.

My own search for a way to make my favourite fruit, the jackfruit, available throughout the year at hotels began at a dinner with Hemant Oberoi, corporate chef of the Taj Group of Hotels. I had read about a special dinner Chef Oberoi had prepared for Michelle and Barack Obama during their stay at the Taj Mahal Palace in Mumbai in 2010 to pay their respects to those who died during the 26/11 terror attack. I reached out to him to see if he could replicate the dinner for some of my clients, and we had a fantastic dining experience at his chef's studio. It was so good that I replicated this dinner several times across India. Each dish served was a signature dish, but the one we couldn't resist requesting a second round of was the Varqui Crab.

Two of our guests first chose the Varqui Kumbh, which used mushroom instead of crab meat, but after seeing our excitement, they also switched to Varqui Crab. That's when I wondered why the chef didn't use raw jackfruit bulb instead of mushroom. Jackfruit has been known as the 'vegetable meat' for centuries, but there was no Varqui Jack on offer. Later, I learned that chefs generally do not use jackfruit in fine dining because of three reasons: the fruit is available only a few months in the year, it is quite messy to handle in the kitchen and the aroma of the fruit is so strong that it can spread quickly in the kitchen. At the dinner in Mumbai, I realized that if chefs in India weren't using jackfruit, then there was no scope of getting it abroad. But I couldn't let go as the health benefits of jackfruit are too numerous to ignore. The wisdom of generations passed on through my maternal uncle, who is now eighty and blind, says: 'A jackfruit tree in the yard extends human life by ten years. During the short season, it works like a bottle brush for your intestinal walls.'

I first experimented with jackfruit burger, based on the success of McDonald's India's veggie burger. Though the burger tasted very good, I soon discovered that the cold chain in India was going to be the weakest link in the supply chain. I remembered the conversation I had with Dr Thomas Koshy during my train ride to Chennai for the visa. He had explained the dehydration process of green pepper for the spice export business he had started. Koshy's son, who now runs the spice business after his father's death, advised me to consider freeze drying as a solution to address my concern about the lack of the cold chain.

When I started experimenting with freeze-dried jackfruit, the former supply chain consultant of i2 within me quickly recognized that the cost of freeze drying offsets the cost of transportation, storage and inventory costs by a big margin. Freeze drying reduces the weight by 82 per cent, you can store the pack in room temperature for 365 days and chefs can configure any dish at the time of consumption since it takes just ten minutes to rehydrate the fruit.

My trials with leading chefs in India and abroad, with whom I had worked closely during my professional career, led to them embracing it with open arms. They surprised me with the range of dishes they prepared. I soon realized that with freeze-dried ripe jackfruit, we can make any dish with apple, and with the raw version, we can make any dish with potato, meat, tofu or cauliflower. More importantly, chefs get a range of options—powdered to make panna cotta, crispy to make oriental fried dishes, tender to make a kathi roll, or paste to make pie or lasagna—by controlling rehydration. This was my moment of serendipity and I dropped the jackfruit burger plan for freeze-dried jackfruit.

Accidental entry to entrepreneurship

As soon as I was convinced about the solution, I started looking for an established player in the food industry to take up this cause since I had no experience in the food sector. I approached Navas Meeran, MD, Eastern Curry Powder, the largest maker of curry powder from Kerala. At the end of my presentation Meeran said, 'James, while you were presenting, I wasn't paying attention to the business case, I was watching your passion to create an organized market for jackfruit. How will you transfer this passion to someone else? In my opinion, if you really want this to take off, you must start it.' Seeing my hesitation, he quickly added, 'The food industry is not as complicated as the software industry and you can always come to me for any advice or help.' His words hit me like a ton of bricks or jackfruits and I instantly connected so many dots in my head.

1. I was at Microsoft's CEO Summit in Seattle and one of the attendees asked Warren Buffet how he got his first funding for investment. Buffet then narrated his meeting with an old man in a plantation. At the end of Buffet a making a good case to invest in a steel company, the old man responded, 'Son, I have no idea what you are talking about,' then paused for a minute and said, 'but I see a genuine passion within you and I think I can trust you, so I will give you the money.'

2. I was going around Kerala and speaking to students about the importance of entrepreneurship. I was mentoring three start-ups operating with very limited resources, and I was shying away from the opportunity to start something on my own.

3. I had gone around the world to acquire the skills to become a global manager and was already in discussions with someone about an Asia-Pacific role I could perform from Kochi. Meeran's comments just opened my eyes and I thought, 'Why don't I try to apply those global skills I acquired for the jackfruit? After all, I am living in the land of jackfruit and it is for a good cause.'

The three start-ups I was mentoring taught me how to leverage social media, crowd sourcing and e-commerce retail channels to keep my investments low at all levels. These lessons, combined with my manufacturing, supply chain, marketing, PR skills and industry contacts, helped me launch my first entrepreneurship venture to create an organized market for jackfruit in less than ten months. The idea of JackFruit365 was an instant hit with the media and I won the Start-up

Entrepreneur of the year award at TiEcon Kerala in our first year. This year, we are entering international markets.

JackFruit365 is anchored on a sound business model to ensure that all my partners benefit from every sale, but we are all in it for a larger social cause, which is why I prefer to call it a social venture.

When I shared this story with my commissioning editor, Anish, he asked me to read *The Alchemist* by Paulo Coelho before I did anything. As I got to the end, I read about Santiego meeting his attackers at the pyramid where he realizes that the treasure is actually at the church where he started the journey. I think my meeting with Meeran was like the scene at the pyramid. Meeran made me realize that the global product I had been after from the time I read the newspaper article was indeed the humble jackfruit in my backyard!

FOUR

START YOUR JOURNEY TO GOD'S OWN OFFICE

MOTIVATION

It is not easy to have a goal to go global and then come back home to a small town, remain content and continue to perform well in one's professional life. One must experience the world to withdraw to a small place and remain happy; otherwise you are always tempted with the notion that the grass is greener on the other side. In hindsight, it was easy for me to go global. The paths were clearly laid in front of me as many Indian professionals my age had already done it, so there was a strong current in my favour. The return journey was not at all easy. Firstly, I had a family and secondly, the current was against me, with several roadblocks and unknown factors like my wife's registration back in India.

1. Conviction

One must have a strong conviction on why you want to come home. In my case, on that foggy morning at the Halfmoon Bay Golf Links, I was posed with a tough choice: Who do I need to settle down with, Bharati or Dhanrati? I was convinced I needed both to be happy.

If Indra Nooyi and Satya Nadella are the poster children of the Indian professional, we all forget that the poster children of our childhood were Mowgli and Shanti from *The Jungle Book*. During the first two decades of their life, Mowgli and Shanti loved Bharati , the well-marinated life in the small towns and villages of India surrounded by nature, spirituality, art, culture and many generations of relatives and friends. Parents, teachers, siblings, extended family members, neighbours, religious leaders—they all had time to inculcate the love for knowledge in us to make us a Bharati. We were constantly reminded of two things.

First, we were relatively very poor in this world and second, education was the only way to upgrade our social status. We sought knowledge in everything we came across in life, be it a comic book like *Amar Chitra Katha,* making a kite, amplifying the sound of country-made firecrackers with coconut shells or old metal vessels, the chemistry of taste by playing around with turmeric, coriander and chilli, permutation and combination from a game of chess, strategies from television serials like *Chanakya, Ramayan* and Bollywood movies, the list goes on.

For two decades, we kept shaking our Bharati—love for knowledge—like a champagne bottle. By the early nineties, the convergence of globalization and the IT revolution brought someone to our doorstep, Dhanrati —love for wealth—looking for the 'cheap genius' within us. That removed the cork of this champagne bottle and unleashed an army of Indian professionals ready to take the reins from the baby boomers. We were excited about the rich dividends of being a part of this ride with Dhanrati—money, responsibilities, access to entertainment and global travel, things we never dreamt of during our childhood.

Now that we have found our own place in the world,

and we need to look back and compare Dhanrati with Bharati, it is really hard to choose. If Bharati is like the Indian thali meal, then Dhanrati is like the delicious chicken tikka served without rice or roti. The former has no specific highlights or star features but you feel pleasant after the meal, while the latter is very exciting, but over time you feel a bit stuffed and uneasy. If Bharati is like riding on a majestic elephant—very slow but so secure that you can even sleep—Dhanrati is like riding a cheetah, faster than anyone else, but one that makes you feel scared as you are afraid to get down. We all agree it is Bharati who got us Dhanrati. However, our children are deprived of Bharati and are riding the cheetah with us, eating chicken tikka for breakfast, lunch and dinner. If baby boomers produced Generation Jones, whose characteristics include lack of optimism, distrust and general cynicism, our choice in this love triangle will define the next two decades for us and the next four decades for our children.

So, do you go by what our yogis would say—'You have tasted the world, now renounce it'—or is there an opportunity to slow down Dhanrati and bring Bharati back into our life? I have the strong conviction that even if it may look tough, it is a goal definitely worth pursuing. You need to introspect as a family and assess if you have a similar conviction to make this journey.

2. Constant focus

Once you have the conviction, you need to constantly focus on your goal for the tide is against you and many risks and temptations will come your way to derail you. To remain constantly aware of my goal, I used a tip I learned at a youth camp in college. The best thing to maintain constant awareness of one's goal is to give him or her a name which is a reminder of the goal. This way, whenever someone calls them, they will be reminded of their goal. Obviously you don't choose your name or change it for this purpose. I found that the next best thing to remind me of my goal was to include it as part of my Windows login password, which I had to type in more often than someone calling my name! As long as I was in the US, my password had something to remind me of my goal to move to the UK. As soon as I landed in the UK, it was changed to remind me of my goal to join Microsoft, then to move to Bangalore and finally to my home town. This constant awareness helped me grab the opportunities as they came my way, like the split-second decision to drop off Michael at the train station and discuss my transfer to India. Or fend off risks that could have stopped me from achieving my goal. Once, I was asked to consider an attractive role in Redmond or in Singapore, and I quickly responded saying that I'd do it only if it could be managed from my home town.

In another instance, during a plane ride from Mumbai to Bangalore, I was chatting with Ravi Venkatesan and he suggested that I travel to Redmond for a meeting as a reward for my good work. I told him that I was moving my family that week, hence I would prefer to go the following year. He was clearly taken aback and didn't like the idea of my moving away to a small town and working from home rather than in the office where he was based. 'I don't think it is good idea, you should be working closely with my office. Who approved it?' he asked. I felt shivers going down my spine as I knew that if I did not derail him from the thought, he would nuke my ten-year plan within minutes. I quickly responded, ' Ravi, when there is an opportunity to work for the best company in the world and live where you grew up, I think it should be given a chance.' He took a deep breath and said, 'I don't know if I fully agree but I think you have a point, give it a try.' A few minutes before he sat down next to me, I had logged in to my laptop and the password was Aluva and a few characters to remind me of the month and the year when I wanted to move.

3. Earn the right to return

One basic principle I learned early on during sales training at 3M was that one should 'earn the right to advance'. This is applicable in customer situations as well as in career moves within an organization. My move from the Bay Area to my home town involved many steps over a long period of time. First and foremost, you should do full justice to your current job for your manager to make an extra effort to support you in a journey different from most people's. For example, in my case, I knew I had established good credibility with the leadership at the Informatica headquarters, especially with my manager Sanjay, and if I told them that I had to move to the UK with or without them, they would try their best to accommodate me. Same was the case in the UK and later in Bangalore.

Professionals who aspire to return to their home

town and remain professionals should consistently work on their unique and signature style till they pass the Mohammed versus Mountain test—you must figure out a way for the mountain to come to you. You must resist the temptation to become a generalist far too soon. Beware, most corporate career-development programmes are designed to fast-track you from a specialist to a general manager where the short-term rewards are very attractive but you lose your unique skill set. This is well articulated by Tom Friedman in his book *That Used to Be US*. Gone are the days when corporations expected professionals to migrate for jobs. Instead, they accept that jobs now need to migrate to wherever the professionals are. Friedman's advice to professionals is to think like an artisan where you are proud to put your signature at the end of every job. The world notices the unique skill you have mastered and the job will migrate to you even if you are in a corner of the world.

You must work hard to pass the Mohammed versus Mountain test before you fail the inchworm test. This must be done before the strength of the parents' roots in their home town grows weaker than the strength of the children's roots. Each time, we managed to move before our children's roots grew deeper wherever we lived. My eldest daughter was one when we moved from the US to the UK; my first two daughters were five and three when moved from the UK to Bangalore; and my three daughters were seven, four and one when we made the final move back.

Once you have passed this Mohammed versus Mountain test, wait for the next opportunity to come your way. You can take advice from all your mentors, but the decision on when to make the move towards your next phase should be yours. Do it only when you are ready. Always remember, 'When an egg is broken from within, a new life begins, but when it is broken from outside, a life is lost.'

The final move from a city to your home town will be the toughest. In case you are not able to find an employer who is willing to take a chance with you, then you should look for employers who have a centre in your home town where you can work from. These will be large Indian corporations with offices in tier-two and tier-three towns. But never sign up for a small regional role for your town as you will soon grow out of the role. If none of this works, as a last resort, start mentoring a number of start-ups in your home town while you are working in the city. Get involved, share your business expertise, help them with your industry connections, and if one of them clicks, you have the opportunity to invest and join them as a partner. Mentoring start-ups is something you should do even if you are able to move with your employer as it helps you in the long run. Once you have got your goal and strategy set, you need to set up your God's Own Office before you make the final move. To me, God's Own Office is a place from where you can work more efficiently than your base office, one that gives you enough positive energy to help you come up with creative ideas for your work, and is logistically well-connected for you to travel on short notice for meetings.

4. Location, location, location

Choosing the right location for your home office is the most important factor, which will make or break your plans to work from there. The most critical aspect for you to work effectively from home is reliable digital connectivity to work without interruption, just like you would work from your office in the city. Remember, it was your decision to work from home and not your employer's, so the onus is on you to make sure you are able to work without interruption, unlike at the office, where the onus is on the IT department. When you are choosing a location in a village or a small town, you must make sure you have more than one option of high bandwidth broadband connection. In metros, you take broadband connections for granted. But in villages, it has not penetrated that well, so you should scout for locations where physical cables are already in place. Do not take promises that cables will be laid for granted. Consumer broadband connections are a lot cheaper in India than office connections; at my home, I have four times better bandwidth than at our local office in Kochi.

You will need to travel to your city office frequently. In my case, I went for meetings to different metros at least seven or eight days a month. In addition, I volunteered to pay for all expenses of travelling and staying in Bangalore as long as the meeting was planned in advance. I did this only to ensure that in case my manager changed, the new manager shouldn't feel that my decision to move to my home town is negatively affecting the expense budget for the whole team. The cost of living in a small town is significantly lower than staying in a metro, and one can easily afford to travel if it is planned well in advance. So, for me, easy access to an airport was the second most critical aspect, whereas for another person I knew, whose office was based in Chennai, easy access to the train station was more important. I managed to find a location within ten minutes from the airport, firstly to ensure that I could get to the airport even if there was a last minute *hartal* or strike in Kerala. It came in handy many times. While my colleagues in the local office who lived in the city had to be dropped at the airport at 4 a.m. for a 7.30 a.m. flight, so that the office taxi agency could get their cars back to their garage before the strike began at 6 a.m., I would reach the airport at 5.50 a.m. as it took only ten minutes for my local taxi to get back home. Another thing I had to ensure was that my location was before any potential traffic hotspots from the airport. Since Kerala, like England, has a lot of rivers, bridges are always major traffic hotspots. Hence, we picked a place before the first bridge.

The third aspect of the location of your God's Own Office is that it should provide enough positive energy for you to stay motivated and enjoy your work. In my case, I draw a lot of energy from nature, spirituality, and friends and family. So we picked an apartment overlooking the Periyar river and the Aluva Shivaratri temple, which was only forty-five minutes away from my ancestral home where many generations of my relatives and friends live. A CEO from Mumbai who had come to my house once said, 'For James, a holiday is only a 90 degree turn of his chair.' At the city office I used to fill my dull moments with water-cooler conversations, tea breaks with colleagues, extended lunches or relaxing on the massage chair. At my God's Own Office, I fill my slow moments watching some brilliant scenes of nature like the courtship dance of snakes or kingfishers, parrots and bulbuls building nests, and chicks taking their first flight. I can watch fish jump over water in the morning and evening. I also get to see the art of fishing by river otters, kites, giant herons, cormorants, pied kingfishers and the local fishermen. Instead of extended lunch breaks at the food court, I have a warm home-cooked lunch. Some days, I take a boat to our adopted farm on an island to check out the progress and bring back some fresh vegetables. I use the eight to ten days I spend across various offices to proactively connect with all my colleagues and maintain a personal connect. I always make sure I take out enough time to catch up with them over lunch or coffee.

Such a location will keep you motivated and you will work extra hard so you can keep working from your God's Own Office

TECHNOLOGY

5. Backup, backup, triple backup!

At God's Own Office, you are your own Chief Information Officer. I said that once at a talk and a young professional asked me, 'Isn't that too much to take on oneself? At work, if something goes wrong with my connection, the IT department will be there to take care of it or to take the blame, while we happily take a break from work.' While I agree that there is no one to fix your problem, it's not that bad if you plan your backups well. The two most critical requirements for uninterrupted work from home are your broadband connection and power supply. Most modern builders will supply high-end bandwidth to the property as part of their specifications at the time of selling. But, some will try to convince you that wireless or Wi-max is the best and the cleanest option at the time of handover. I fell into the trap first, but then I did a dry run before I moved my office to the property. During the dry run, I realized that the bandwidth they offered was the best-case scenario and the actual bandwidth kept oscillating significantly every minute. During voice calls over the Internet, the sound would go from loud to mute several times. Moreover, the possibility of interference with other wireless devices at home was very high. I insisted on getting the physical cable as per the contract. In addition, I got a backup connection from the state telecom department, and my third backup was the USB wireless connection I use when travelling. The optimal way to manage these connections is to have a high bandwidth, high volume data plan with the most reliable network, and a high bandwidth, low volume data plan for the second connection as you only need it for a short time during outages. If both fail for a short time, you get downgraded to the level of an employee on travel with your wireless connection, which most people are used to as a temporary measure. But if both connections are down for a longer time, like when major civic work near my place led to both lines being cut for eight hours,

I go to my extended office, a hotel room near my home, which is my final backup plan.

Most modern housing complexes, even in small towns, offer generator backup in case of power failure. Even if the generator backup kicks in within seconds or minutes, this short gap still kills your broadband connection if the modem goes off. You need a third power backup to cover your connection for this short yet frequent disruption due to the sad state of power in India. Invest in a low-capacity UPS, which will give you enough uninterrupted power for all modems and phones. Moreover, the UPS acts as a good voltage stabilizer and gives protection from power surges. I once had a power surge within a month of moving in and all our equipment, except those connected through the UPS, had to be repaired. Unfortunately, I had plugged my laptop charger straight into a socket and, during the power surge, it got burned. Since then, all work-related stuff, including my cell phone charger, is connected through the small UPS. Finally, make sure that all critical support staff in your building know that you work from home and that they need to maintain a minimum stock of diesel. They also need to have the cash and authority to replenish the diesel before it runs out.

6. Technologies for remote working at God's Own Office

Once you have taken care of all connectivity issues at your home with triple backup, you need to make sure you have all the technology required to work as efficiently as you would from office.

First and foremost, you should have the ability to collaborate effortlessly with your colleagues from your home. Most corporations of medium and large size have enterprise-grade collaboration technology already in place; others should secure permission to use consumer-grade technology which is free and equally effective. I will focus on the functionalities rather than the specific technology.

Presence information: Your online presence is more important than your physical presence in an office. When you work from home, your colleagues have no clue whether you are in your office or not. You should have the ability to let your colleagues know if you are logged in so that anyone can contact you. Technologies to track presence information will automatically show an indicator against your name: green means you are online and free of any meetings, red means you are online but in a meeting and orange means you are away from your computer. Most email systems integrate this presence information and when an email arrives, you can see if the sender is currently online and, if free, you need not send a lengthy reply. Instead, you can have real-time interactive discussions and close the case a lot quicker.

Instant messenger for real-time interaction: If both parties are online and available, instant messenger allows you to open a chat window and exchange brief information, just like you would using other consumer messenger apps. This technology is also very helpful when you are in meetings or on conference calls as you can interact with someone else without disturbing others in the meeting.

Online audio and video conferencing: Sometimes you can't resolve issues by exchanging information through just text messages. At work, you would walk over to a person's desk or pick up the phone if the person is not in your own office building. Online audio- and video-conferencing technology allows you to upgrade your text chat to an audio or video call with the click of a button, like a Skype call. Most of the time, I only use audio calls. I use video calls only if my colleagues insists on seeing the view from my place, or if it is a new employee whom I haven't met before. Video calls need a lot of bandwidth, so use them only if it is a must.

Desktop sharing: I find this to be a lot more effective than sitting across a table with a sheet of paper. With one click, you can share your screen with your colleague and both of you can look at the same screen. More importantly, since the sound also comes from the same place, you can concentrate on work. If required, you can give control to the other person, who can make changes to your document during the discussion.

Remote access to your organization's network: The ability to remotely connect to your corporate applications and execute tasks like approving leave, expenses, purchase orders, etc. is the next big requirement. You cannot go to your office if something urgent comes up, which requires you to be logged in to your corporate network. This is widely available in all companies with varying degrees of ease of access. It is best if your organization allows direct access without going through a VPN connection.

A cloud to keep your data: Information is power, but

it can also become a ball and chain which can tie you down to your computer all the time. When working from home, you should adopt a culture of sharing information proactively with your colleagues. This will reduce the number of requests you get for a document, which would require you to connect to your PC and attach files from there. There are various provisions for employees to share their documents in a shared space or in the cloud, which others can access if you give them permissions. This will save you a lot of time as your colleagues will develop the habit of searching for the information there before contacting you. In case they still contact you, can manage that from your phone itself with a link to the folder they can access. This approach will not only save you time, it will also save you bandwidth. This approach is also your best safety backup and decreases your dependence on your office laptop. This habit helped me when we had the power surge that destroyed my laptop battery charger. It took two days to get a new charger, but I was able to work from my personal computer with temporary permission to access my files in the shared folders. The new term for this shared space is called the cloud. Most corporations have a private cloud concept within their security firewalls and there are various public cloud options available for smaller firms.

Finally, you must have a smartphone with spell-check and permission to access email, calendar, contacts, etc.

Here is an example of how I used the collaboration technology to work with a colleague from another country and quickly turn a crisis situation into significant victory.

I got a call from Anuradha, who works at the magazine *CFO India*, at 8 p.m. one day when I was at my home. I was showing my kids a firefly which had flown up to our balcony on the tenth floor.

'James, we have a situation. Due to the political unrest in Thailand, we have to move our CFO Leadership Conclave from Bangkok to Kuala Lumpur. Can you still provide support?'

She needed to make a decision on the new venue within twenty-four hours as we were less than a month away from the event. I had a unique experience planned in Bangkok, which was relevant to the topic of discussion. I was clueless on what to do in Kuala Lumpur and we did not have enough time to research and plan something from scratch.

I immediately went online and, from our organization chart, I navigated down to my counterpart in the Malaysian subsidiary to set up a call in the morning and check if he had any advice for me. Luckily, I saw the green button next to his name, meaning he was online and free. Great news for me, but not so much for his family as it was 10.30 p.m. there. The green button is from a wonderful collaboration technology called unified communication. My lifeline for more than four years, it allowed me to work from my home in Aluva more effectively than from my office in Bangalore.

I clicked the green button, opened a chat window and typed, 'Hi Deng, I am your counterpart in India and need help. Do you have a few minutes to chat?' He replied, 'Hi James, I can chat for a few minutes.'

I conveyed my situation to Deng and he responded, 'Can you talk? I may have just the thing for you.' I immediately closed the door to my room and put my jawbone headset on, which is clever enough to mute the mike when my mouth is shut. One more click and we upgraded the chat to a voice call.

Deng said, 'James, your topic is cloud computing. Do you want to take the CFOs to the cloud for this

At the Circle of Excellence Awards ceremony with
Steve Ballmer (*extreme left*)

A jackfruit in a pack for 365 days

My primary office at my residence—a vacation
is only a 90-degree turn of my chair away

My backup office at the attic of our cottage
where I work when we have guests

The view during the monsoon floods

We get fresh fish caught in front of us from Sivan's shop

A coat hanger from IKEA London repurposed to hang banana bunches while they turn ripe

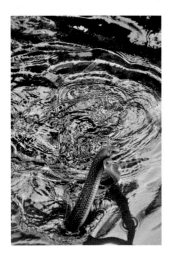

Snakes in love: two hearts

meeting?' I responded: 'I would love to, but I think you are pulling my leg.' He said, 'No, I am not kidding. There is this unique venue on the forty-second floor of the Petronas Towers called Malaysian Petroleum Club, which is always surrounded by clouds. I was planning to host a meeting there for CEOs which got cancelled.' I was slightly sceptical. 'This sounds great, but I don't know if I can afford it,' I said.

With another click, Deng shared his desktop and I could see the full cost break up he had prepared for his meeting. It was well within my budget. I told him that it was perfect, he fired a mail to his agency whose CEO was a member of this exclusive club, and I added the date, time and number of people.

Within eight minutes of Anuradha's call, I had another spectacular experience in the works for my CFOs. The next day, at 8 a.m., I got a confirmation email saying that the venue was available and they had blocked it for me. By 9 a.m. the next morning, the *CFO India* team was thrilled to hear that I was not only supporting the conclave in Kuala Lumpur, but had an idea which would be the highlight of the event.

Thanks to the huge non-resident Indian community

from Kerala, I could take a short flight from Kochi to Kuala Lumpur via Singapore. The CFOs from metros didn't get any sleep since either their flights were at 3 a.m. or they had long stopovers. Though I had a kid sitting next to me who tried to keep me awake, I still got some time to catch up on sleep before the group arrived in Kuala Lumpur.

The meeting went so well that the editor of *CFO India* decided to publish a feature article called *Cloud9 for CFOs*.

By the way, with this technology, your kids might find it a bit strange to see you stick your head into the laptop, murmur, laugh loudly and occasionally shout. My kids think it is the XBox equivalent of what grown-ups play at work!

7. Soundproof—only you need to know your secret

A year after I moved back to my home town, I was having a late-night debriefing at a bar at the Taj Mahal Palace in Mumbai with a few members of our senior leadership from India. It had been a hectic day for everyone and a great one for me as I had successfully concluded a CFO Forum with the top CFOs from India, including Microsoft's Corporate CFO. After nine months of hard work, including two major shocks—first the date getting postponed and then our star CFO resigning weeks before the meeting date—I still managed to land a great meeting. The meeting set the stage for a series of executive engagements with CFOs in India. We were all celebrating and, during a lighter moment, I shared a little secret: 'When the CFOs team landed in Mumbai to check out the venue, I got a call and I was actually getting a jackfruit from the tree on my farm.' One of the executives responded: 'Where is your farm in Bangalore, I would like to see.' I said, 'My farm is near Kochi. I live there, not in Bangalore.' He couldn't believe it. I had got myself into a similar situation like I had when I was taking the flight with Ravi. Eventually, when he found out that I had been doing this for a while, he said, 'We do so many things together, and I still didn't notice that you've moved. It must be a good thing.' Later, I was playing golf with a group of customer executives—one of the most expensive golf games as far as I was concerned. I flew down on a Saturday at my own expense to my office base in Bangalore for a round of golf with our top customers, and we didn't even play a round of golf; it was just training for beginners. After training, all of us sat down for the networking lunch and the topic of me working out of God's Own Office came up. It went into a heated discussion as many were against it. Eventually, one of the technology executives from an MNC shared some statistics on a study they had conducted on why working from home doesn't suit their employees in India. Ambient noise was the number one issue faced by employees who tried to work from home. Their customers and colleagues got annoyed when they heard vehicles honking, dogs barking, kids crying or some construction work in the background. Many employees considered these noises normal when they were at home. Then my colleague said, 'The only noise we hear from James's end is birds chirping and we tell him not to close the window.'

Stay in the cloud: I reluctantly chose to work out of a flat most of the time rather than an independent house so that I wouldn't need to worry about security, utilities outages, etc. when I was travelling on business. I picked the top floor for two reasons. One, it gave me the best view of the river and two, we hated people living above us because of a bad experience in Dallas where we had a child constantly jumping on the floor above us. There, the floors are wooden and sound insulation is really poor, which is not the case with concrete floors in India. However, we did not want to risk a repeat of the Dallas experience. Choosing the top floor cut me off from all road noises as well, which is anyway not much if you live in a small town or village. In my case, the sound of fishermen slapping the water with their oars to make the fish leave their hideout is more frequent than cars honking. Additionally, being on the top floor saved me from the noise from the children's park on the ground floor.

Stay away from a flight path now and in the future: When I lived in Las Vegas, my brother used to keep track of the expansion plans of the Vegas airport. He used to tell me that his house price would tank if a new runway put his house under the flight path. I didn't really understand the gravity of his comment till our first night back in India. At 3 a.m., my wife and I woke up to the horrific sound of a cargo plane almost scraping past the chimney of my cousin's house. We both looked at each other and asked, 'How can they sleep with this noise?' While one could get used to such a situation, your customers or colleagues may not, and may get annoyed. So, make sure you study the current and future flight paths in your area and avoid them as much as possible. In our case, we picked a location parallel to the runway. Still, a plane to Colombo flies over our head during take off once a week, which is not as bad as a plane landing.

Two doors of separation from your loved ones: When I started working from God's Own Office, my youngest daughter was only eighteen months old. In the morning, when I entered my home office, she used to say 'bye-bye' to me as if she had figured out that when I went into that room, I was as good as out of the house! She wouldn't even bother to knock on my door as, over time, she learned that there would be no response. But kids are kids and sometimes they can't control themselves. Nor is there any point in trying to control them. They won't be able to understand the importance of your conference call with someone they can't see. In such situations, I would go to my balcony and close the door, which gave me two doors of separation so she could do whatever she wanted without disturbing me.

For worst case scenarios, find a hotel nearby: Spend at least a week in the area before deciding on the location, and check out all the religious establishments near your God's Own Office as well as their major festival calendars. Usual suspects are mosques, churches and temples. With mosques, prayers are held every Friday but the time is fixed, so you can block your calendar to do some other activity when the loudspeaker is switched on. With churches and temples, the frequency is less but the intensity of noise could be beyond your control. I was once on a call with the speech writer of our COO in the US. Just before it was my turn to speak, fireworks went off at our local church to mark their annual festivities. He was calling out my name to speak, but if I had turned on the mike, they would have thought a bomb had exploded nearby. So, I sent a message to another colleague on the call to go before me and waited for the fireworks to end. Afterwards, I marked that date on my calendar to make sure I checked into a hotel near the airport beforehand. It's good to have a tie up with one hotel where you can meet people, especially colleagues or customers who occasionally come to your town and you are the only one they know there.

It's more practical to meet them at a hotel closer to you than inviting them to your home or going to the city hotel where they are staying. Over time, you will build a relationship with the hotel, even if you are not a big customer for them. In worst case scenarios, like fireworks or broadband outages, I book a room and work from there. I've only had to do so twice in five years, but it is good to have an option in such scenarios.

For further soundproofing, you can invest in a Jawbone headset, which will shut off all background noises when you are not speaking.

WORK

8. Discipline: Be Khushwant Singh on weekdays and Shashi Tharoor on weekends

Many professional contacts warned me about the productivity loss I would face if I moved back to a small town. Not because of technology or infrastructure gaps, but from frequent disruptions by the people around you in a village. Whatever pattern and discipline you would like to follow, start from day one. People may find it difficult at the beginning, but they will quickly accept it and work around your schedule.

Behave like the late Khushwant Singh during weekdays: When you work from home, that too in a village, the number one challenge is people dropping in to say hello. They assume that if you had important things to do, you would be at work, not home. First, I explained the concept of conference calls to my brother, sister and very close relatives. Even then, initially I had to avoid a few people who were driving past my place. While it caused some irritation in the beginning, they soon realized that I am not selective and am equally unkind to everyone. They reluctantly accepted that a disruption to a conference call could cost me my job. Since I worked for a multinational corporation based in the US, there was no guaranteed time when I would be free. Within two months, I started getting advance calls from people to see if I would be travelling on a specific date and, if not, whether I could free up my calendar to meet them. That was easy to manage even though it doesn't happen that often in a small town as most people usually make last-minute social decisions. Bad news spreads faster in villages and all my distant relatives soon got to know about my rude constraints.

Like Khushwant Singh, I have given clear instructions to our building security staff: 'Don't let anyone ring my bell unless you know that I am expecting them.' I usually tell the staff in advance if I am expecting someone. The only exceptions are the postman and courier people because if I miss them, it will cost me dearly. The postman normally brings bad news from authorities, like a disconnection notice, which I need to sign, and the courier guy brings stuff redirected from my office, which is usually a few days late already. Others get a standard response: 'Sir is in a phone meeting till late night. Please leave your number and message, sir will call you back.' I usually call them back promptly so that they don't have to make another trip. This discipline helped me after my jackfruit venture got a lot of news coverage. Many people travelled from other districts to get a hold of me, some even showed up at my wife's hospital to track me down. My security staff took care of the situation, taking down phone numbers and sending them away. Nearly 90 per cent of the visitors wanted to sell jackfruits, which are in abundant supply, while others wanted me to focus on their favourite fruit or flower. I would return all the calls during my morning walk the next day.

Behave like Shashi Tharoor during weekends: Like UN diplomat-turned-politician Shashi Tharoor, I would attend every family function possible during the weekends. Unlike other relatives, I would ensure that I wasn't bothered while I was there unless something went seriously wrong. Whenever I went on vacation, I gave two-weeks' notice to all my key colleagues and a reminder three days before I left. I did this so that they would feel slightly apologetic if they had to call me during my vacation. A colleague once said that she gets more stressed out before my vacation than before her own!

I moved back to my home town because I value a life surrounded by many generations of family and friends. I really enjoy attending baptisms, birthdays, holy communions, weddings, anniversaries, house warmings and church, temple or village festivals like Onam, snake boat race, etc.—but only as long as they are on a weekend. The only exception to this rule is funerals of close relatives or friends. On Sundays, I wear our traditional dhoti and go to church like a villager who has never left town. It is an absolute pleasure to stand at the back and watch my kids stand in line in front along with their Sunday school classmates and being scolded by priests and nuns like I used to be. I play the same role I saw my dad and uncles play when I was growing up, copying everything they did— participating in mission Sunday auctions, Christmas carols, collecting holy palm leaf on passion Sunday, Passover meals on Monty Thursday, watching kids shriek when they drink the bitter green juice on Good Friday and taking a long walk from my wife's family church to my family church.

9. Out of sight, not out of mind

When I discussed my plan to work from my home town with a senior colleague in the Bangalore office, his first reaction was, 'James, out of sight means out of mind.' He cautioned me that I would lose touch with other colleagues, especially with the leadership team, and I would lose out in the long run. Even though I had seen many of my colleagues in the US and the UK work from home efficiently, these comments from a seasoned manager in India did shake my confidence somewhat. But they also inspired me to proactively work out a strategy to make sure that I remained in the minds of my colleagues and leadership team.

Top of the mind for leadership team: To ensure that I stayed close to the leadership team, I switched to a role in our team that provided the most visibility. It involved strengthening the relationship with the top executives of our customers. These executives are always going to be a top priority for the leadership team, and if I was their channel for interacting with these executives, I would also stay on top of everyone's minds. More importantly, whenever Steve Ballmer or one of his direct reports visited India, I had a significant role to play as they also liked to meet the top executives of top customers in the country.

Top of the mind for colleagues in all offices: As part of my agreement to work from my home town, I had volunteered to work from the Bangalore office during the first week of every month from Tuesday to Thursday at my own expense. Those who work from one office have water-cooler conversations with colleagues and participate in social activities in that office. However, their interaction with colleagues from other offices is very limited. I used this to my advantage and worked out a strategy that would help me achieve a better relationship with employees from all offices. Whenever I had meetings in one city,

I would take the first flight there and return by the last flight the next day. This gave me at least two full days in that city and I would work from our offices there before and after my meeting. Whenever I worked from those offices, I would catch up with colleagues over coffee or lunch.

In addition, I had a network of service apartments in these cities and, if there was a social event, like quarterly employee parties or a training programme, I would check out from my hotel and move to the service apartment. This was less expensive and I could extend my stay at the office that week. Sometimes, if we had a new hire for a critical customer, I would use this extended stay as an opportunity for that. This approach helped me to counter the reduction in face time with my colleagues in Bangalore with more face time with colleagues from other offices.

I signed up for responsibilities that involved coordinating with a large number of employees. For example, the annual planning process involved almost every division and a lot of employees. I took the responsibility to coordinate planning for the largest business group, which meant a lot of them had to work with me for a good two months. I would also make an extra effort to ask questions during calls with all employees and respond to announcements on email to make sure that everyone knew I was tuned into company affairs. I would also attend all team activities and off-sites in India and at our headquarters to ensure that I had a good connect with all my colleagues.

10. Be a local ambassador

Once you have secured approval from your current manager, you also need to make sure your future manager won't reverse that decision. This is possible if the leadership team of your organization sees an extra benefit of you working from your home town. I looked at the options of moving to a role which gave me responsibilities for my region. However, when I consulted a few friends who had tried that in the past, I realized it is not a long term solution, even if you are willing to take a pay cut. Regional field roles are usually meant for youngsters beginning their career. Most people exhaust the role in two or three years and move on to bigger roles. Unless the manager is exceptionally mature, he or she could feel uncomfortable with a senior colleague working for them. Most customers and partners would also like to see a new face in a couple of years to repair any damaged relationship, which is inevitable if you are driven by targets.

Over time, I realized that it was best to take no direct responsibilities for my region. Instead, I would act as a helping hand for anyone trying to do something big in my state, while keeping my national role intact. To make it legitimate in HR parlance, I added one goal to my commitments: 'Volunteer time to improve Microsoft's favourability in Kerala.' That was an easy one to get approval for as my state was known to be less favourable towards Microsoft at that time. I started building a relationship with the business community by lending expertise as an executive sponsor for some of the big customers. Many senior entrepreneurs from Kerala also took morning flights and we bumped into each other at the airport lounge or in the plane, which gave me many opportunities to interact with them. I also offered a helping hand to our marketing team to host CEO roundtables in my town on their behalf. In addition, the local team got me to speak at conferences when they couldn't get people to fly down from HQ. Speaking at conferences brought me closer to policy makers and government officials in Kerala, who were either fellow speakers or organizers. Many of them were caught between the devil and the deep sea. On one hand, they wanted prestigious corporations like Microsoft to expand their operations to Kerala, provide employment for the youth and unleash the power of technology in the state. On the other hand, some members of their political leadership wanted to prevent anyone from using Microsoft technology in the state. They were pleasantly surprised to find that there was someone from Kerala who was close to the Microsoft India leadership and was living in the state. They felt that I could be a bridge between the two parties and suggested that I play an active role in improving the relationship.

I worked closely with Microsoft India chairman Bhaskar Pramanik's office and Chief Minister Oommen Chandy's office to identify areas where both parties could work together. Bhaskar assigned me as his ambassador for the state, which meant that I would accompany him to every meeting in Kerala. He also assigned Kerala as a priority state for himself. I had to work across various divisions at Microsoft to come up with a strategy for Kerala while the chief minister's office worked with various ministries. After a year, we had a kick off meeting at Kerala House in Delhi with the chief minister, senior cabinet ministers, Bhaskar and heads of various divisions to discuss an action plan for both parties.

The best part of being an ambassador is that you enjoy organizational immunity! Both parties know that your salary or bonus does not depend on your role as ambassador since you have another day job. Hence, they both treat you well and do not hold you responsible for the final outcome. But the biggest incentive for me was that the Microsoft leadership team had an interest in keeping me at my God's Own Office. Both parties appreciated the genuine sincerity I showed in bringing them together. The relationship I built with the policy makers and entrepreneurs from Kerala helped me even after I left Microsoft. When I was toying with the idea of creating an organized market for jackfruit, all of them came forward to offer me encouragement and mentorship and actively promoted my idea at various forums.

One area I consciously avoided was the local media as I really enjoyed the quiet, private life of being a small fish in a small pond. Towards the final year, a local business magazine, *Dhanam*, found out about this farmer-cum-Microsoft man flying under their radar. Since I had already decided to promote the idea of professionals moving back to their home town, I agreed to an interview. *Dhanam* made that into a cover story and the *Economic Times* followed it up with another cover story. Thereafter, everyone knew my secret. I then started writing guest articles for magazines and newspapers. Once I launched JackFruit365, I was everywhere because of the fruit's wide appeal across India. My advice would be to use media wisely if it helps you and your employer, but make sure you have permission from your PR department as it can get out of hand.

11. Adopt start-ups to secure your future

I was asked to join a group of NASSCOM executives for a meeting in Thiruvananthapuram, and had the opportunity to interact with around 800 final-year engineering students from across Kerala. During that interaction, then NASSCOM chairman Rajendra Pawar asked how many of them planned to work in Kerala and how many planned to work outside. About 70 per cent wanted to work outside Kerala and 30 per cent wanted to work in the state.

Later, Pawar discussed this data with the chief minister and other government officials and said that this ratio needed to reverse for the long-term health of the state, which would otherwise run out of its youth. When we discussed this issue, it was clear that most students do not feel confident about finding suitable jobs in Kerala, and that would change only if major corporations invested in the state. For major corporations to invest in Kerala, there has to be a great pool of mid-level managers with ten or more years of experience keen to relocate to the state. Every mid-level manager can hire and train another ten fresh graduates. As a first step, Pawar suggested, Kerala should run a campaign similar to its successful 'God's Own Country' tourism campaign to attract mid-level managers of Keralite origin back to the state.

This situation can be applied to any Indian state without a large metropolis. There is an urgent need for all small towns to retain their fresh graduates and mid-level professionals can play a big role in this. Middle to senior-level professionals have good industry experience and are well connected to critical decision makers and potential investors. However, one's family's financial commitments may not allow us to leave our current jobs to experiment with new business ideas. While you are working from your God's Own Office or even when you are still in the city office, get involved and support the start-up ecosystem in your small town. Look for fresh start-ups working on business ideas closer to your area of expertise, mentor them and introduce them to your industry contacts. As and when you find the business model to be attractive, you could invest as an angel investor with the intention of joining the start-up when it reaches a stage where you can financially afford to leave your current job for a secure income through the start-up. This is a win-win approach for both parties. Professionals can secure your future plan of staying back in your home town. Young entrepreneurs can piggyback on the expertise and contacts of the professionals to kick-start their venture.

FAMILY

12. Safety first . . . your spouse is your safety officer

When you live in a village, you have to be your own Chief Safety Officer. There is no reliable emergency helpline, and even if there is one, don't expect the response to be as prompt as you need. In villages in India, the chances of you dying from stampede, drowning, snake bite or a natural calamity are greater than from a road accident. So, you shouldn't be naive and always choose the least risky option that suits you and your partner. For example, since my childhood, I developed a fear about stampedes at crowded places, especially religious gatherings.

My wife is afraid of water sports and anything other than a pedal boat is beyond her comfort zone. In India, the overall adherence to safety standards is inadequate.

However, my wife likes to be at festivals—both religious and cultural—when the energy and excitement is at the peak since being in the middle of it really gives you an elevated feeling. I am okay if it is just the two of us, but with kids involved, the risk level changes. The solution we have found is to go to such places the evening before the main day. The church, temple or the festival ground will be at its best an evening prior to the main day. Plus, it won't be crowded. This is the best time to take pictures and the safest time to pray without the fear of a stampede. If you are still keen to see the enthusiasm of the crowd, just scroll through TV channels from the comfort of your home. I had imported a kayak from the US while living in the UK and had a great time rowing on the Thames during lunch break at work or early mornings on weekends so I could enjoy the company of beautiful swans and expensive house boats. I took it out once on the Periyar river, which is not tamed with locks and check dams like the Thames. The kayak is now stored away as an emergency rescue device in case of a tsunami after my wife vetoed my hobby.

Another thing one should also pay attention to is the security staff in the building. Get involved in the hiring process, do thorough background checks and once they've been hired, treat them with a lot of respect. They are the first line of defence for your family when you are travelling on business. Paying genuine respect to them gets you more loyalty and they will watch out for your safety like a family member. My relationship with the security staff and others at my apartment was put to test when we had an emergency flooding situation.

It was a Saturday when I woke up to see the Periyar all muddy and risen to a level higher than normal, but nowhere close to the peak level we had seen a few weeks ago. I could see a family of otters struggling to swim upstream as the flow was too fast, especially for the two young ones. The strategy they used was to swim close to the shore, which was near our flat. They spotted a lot of fish in the small opening of the river near our flat, which we had created as part of a bird bath project. Though it got us into serious trouble with the locals, the birds and turtles would treat it as their infinity pool and a family of kingfishers and water hens quickly made it their home. It was a real treat to watch the otters have a feast and see how they carefully escorted their babies to safety.

On Monday, I woke up at 6 a.m. to see something dramatic. The Siva temple was under water. And when I looked down, I noticed that the water had reached our compound wall and was rising. In another two feet, it would reach the ventilation opening on top of our basement parking area. By 7 a.m., it was clear that the water level would cross that mark and our basement would be flooded. I had only two hours to either block the ventilation or limit the damage from the flooding. The basement had a lot of cars, a water purification plant, several pumps and two lifts. My relationship with our support staff, the builder and vendors were put to the test. By 8 a.m., it was clear that we wouldn't be able to block ten grilled ventilations for two reasons. Plywood shops wouldn't be open for another hour, and we could clearly see snakes in the water, making it too risky to stand there while blocking the ventilation. The only option now was to contain the damage.

Within the next hour, we had a team of people from a nearby project site, thanks to a prompt response from the builder. We were able to remove all cars, fill up the overhead tanks before removing the pumps, raise all lifts to the tenth floor and cut off power supply to the basement and the lifts. By 9 a.m., the water level breached the ventilation and within an hour, we had seven feet of water in our basement, which is half the size of a football pitch. I was alone with my kids, so I had to oscillate between the work in the basement and our apartment on the tenth floor without lifts.

There was more work to be done as the water level was still rising and the threat of more dams being opened was still in the air. By evening, we had everything under control. There was no disruption to power, water, phone lines and one set of lifts was restored by next morning. With the help of our loyal staff, we were able to ensure that everyone was safe and we managed to avoid significant property damage during an emergency situation that arises once in sixty years.

13. Children: Locally committed but globally competent

One of the difficult choices parents have to make while moving to Bharat is whether you are sacrificing your children's future by your whacky idea of leaving the modern world. Turn the clock backwards by several decades of development. Are you being selfish by chasing your childhood surroundings at the expense of your children's chance to grow up competing with the big league in the cities? Those who grew up in villages know the struggle one has to go through to prove one's merit in the big cities. I was completely out of place at 3M compared to my colleagues, who were brought up in English 'speaking' schools, while I was brought up in an English 'writing' school. At the age of thirty-six, I had to take accent training in the UK to figure out that I used to pronounce V and W the wrong way. And whenever I would say 'I can't', people would hear 'I can', which got me into trouble many times. Why should you put your children through the same trouble, embarrassment and learning curves that you had to go through when you have a choice which your own parents never had?

This a tough one. On one hand, you are convinced about the all-round benefit Bharati can give your children by riding on the slow and secure mighty elephant, but they will have to make the struggle of leaving the elephant and jumping on to the cheetah like we did. On the other hand, if they continue on the cheetah with us, they will have learned to tame the cheetah even if they couldn't soak up a lot of Bharati. My wife and I debated a lot on this. We weighed the pros and cons of sending them to the only posh international-standard school at our local town and finally arrived at a solution to make them locally committed and globally competent.

Spoken language: While we were living abroad, we

always spoke our mother tongue Malayalam at home so that our children learned our language. They learned correct English from school and friends. After moving back to Kerala, we swapped that policy. We speak English at home while they learn fluent Malayalam from school and friends. Now, even our youngest daughter who was born in India speaks fluent English and has acquired correct accent from my wife, who has the V and W in their respective places. We realized that we had taken this a little too far when a priest from my family, the principal of a school, visited us and, after playing with my children for some time, asked me, 'Which school are you sending your younger daughter. She can't even count to 100?' I was taken aback as she counts very well to 100 and beyond. Later, I realized that he had asked her a question which she was expected to answer in Malayalam, which she didn't know. When I asked the same question, she answered quickly in English. He made us realize that they also need to learn counting in Malayalam if they are to go to buy goods in local shops, and we took corrective action.

Eating etiquette: On most days, we eat traditional dishes and follow the local way of eating. However, we proactively prepare Western dishes once in a while so that they don't forget how to use a knife and fork. In addition, whenever we go out to eat, we tend to order Western dishes for our kids. But we also make sure they are equally comfortable eating the traditional thali meal if we are travelling through remote parts of India.

International exposure: To make sure that our kids are comfortable interacting with children and adults from within and outside India, we plan our holidays with an emphasis on their exposure to the outside world. Kerala, being one of the top ten international destinations, always gets a lot of domestic and international tourists matching our profile. Many properties that are considered luxury holidays for mid-level professionals are a short drive for us. Since we don't have to pay the extra cost of travelling, we can stay there more often than people who live in cities or abroad. At times, we don't even stay and return home the same night. For example, the best beach in Kochi is thirty minutes from our place and we have a day package scheme with a couple of resorts there. We leave after breakfast, check in, change and hit the beach. Then we come back for a lavish lunch and hit the beach again. In the evening, we freshen up and return home. We get a great beach holiday at the fraction of the cost. We can plan it based on the weather and I can say that our kids get international exposure to an extent that they won't giggle if they see a bikini-clad woman at Miami Beach.

To further increase their interaction with children from cities, we select family holiday destinations frequented by professionals working in the nearby metros of Bangalore or Chennai. At such locations, you can plan joint holidays with old friends from the cities.

When city people come home, we go to cities: Since we live in a village, during long holidays we take our kids to the cities for them to get a feel of the place. They now show the same excitement visiting city monuments and big shopping malls as they used to show when we would go for a holiday to a beach or a jungle resort while we were in Bangalore. I use the same service apartments in the cities when I travel for meetings and try to get the best drivers whom I have hired in the past to remove any uncertainties from the trip. Once in four years, we take our kids abroad to places where we lived. This way, we visit our siblings and they get a feel of the world outside.

Traditional local convent schools: Once we had a plan to manage language, etiquette and exposure, we decided to send our children to a traditional local convent school run by a reputed educational institution. The school was more popular for its values and academic excellence than the international school. We wanted our children to integrate well with children of all economic and social backgrounds. International schools treat parents like customers. They respect your time and try to make an extra effort to make life easy for you. However, your children live in a selective and insulated group, which is not a true representation of the world they need to live in. Traditional schools are very demanding for parents. Since my wife had taken some forced time off, thanks to the Indian bureaucracy, she was able to step in and commit a lot of time. I took that role once she started working. Most parents are quite happy to get an admission and will drop everything else for any demands from the school. But that may not be feasible for many of us, who are slaves to our own work calendar. One parent should consider taking some time off and getting involved with school activities till your kids have settled in well and you have built a good rapport with the school management and teachers. During the initial years, my wife was an active parent at school to an extent that she even ended up participating in a dance recital after some fifteen years.

When you live in a small town, it's always better to keep a very low profile among teachers and other parents. Nobody from the school, except the principal, had any indication about my professional life until I started my jackfruit venture. As the local ambassador for Microsoft, I used to get invited as the chief guest or keynote speaker at several educational institutions. The principals who received and introduced me to students sometimes come as chief guests to my children's school. I consciously stay away from making any contact and try to melt into the crowd to avoid any special attention at the school. Living like a small fish in a small pond is the best thing you can do to help your children integrate well with other students and teachers. This doesn't mean that you shouldn't watch out for your children's safety. You still ought to enforce your red lines on discipline and provide constructive feedback for improvements to teachers and the school management.

14. Get involved in helping people around you

While living in a small town, one good thing you can do is share your knowledge with people around you and help them. They will benefit more from your experience than from the little money you can share with them. If you show genuine concern for them, they will help you in ways that your money cannot provide. For example, I give career advice to children in our neighbourhood, which also keeps me in the good books of the many government employees I regularly interact with. We also spend time and money at an orphanage for differently abled children. During our last visit, when we were about to leave, the head of the school showed us five medals they won during the special Olympics in Australia a few months ago! The first time I had seen Olympic medals was in London when Sir Mathew Pinsent, a four-time Olympic gold medallist, was the speaker for a Microsoft event. The highlight of his talk was when he took out all four gold medals from an equally impressive medal box. He passed them around for all us to touch. Our children know many kids at the orphanage by their first name and they set aside gift money they get during special occasions for the orphanage.

My wife, being a doctor, tries to help people with medical conditions around us.

The advantage of being charitable in the village was that I could personally verify if the cases were genuine.

One case I remember is about Thanga, wife of Moothakarumban. They lived with their son close to my tiny cottage, which I use as my office when we have guests at home or during school holidays. Their son helped out with painting the cottage and is a handyman I can always count on. Thanga worked in the nearby houses either in the kitchen or in the farm and supported her family with her daily wages. Moothakarumban was old and unable to go to work, so he took care of a small vegetable garden around his laterite brick house.

One day Thanga's son told me, 'Sir, the doctor has said my mother has advanced cancer. Since we are from a poor family, he is advising us to not spend money on an operation as it is already too late.' I couldn't believe that a person I had been seeing for almost a year, always running from one house to another looking content, could disappear in six months. She looked quite healthy and I couldn't understand why the doctor wouldn't take a chance on her. My wife looked at Thanga's medical records and her health and told me that she felt Thanga could live for at least ten more years if she was treated. We intervened and told her son to start treatment at our expense, which the doctor finally agreed to. Demands for more money kept on coming from the hospital. I had just attended a session by Hans Rosling at our worldwide CEO summit in Seattle, where he claimed that Kerala was ahead of even Washington DC in healthcare. And here I was, seeing a family unable to provide care for this poor woman. It had even started hurting my own financial plans.

Then I found out that this family shouldn't be spending a single penny for her treatment. All they had to do was get a below-poverty-line (BPL) card. Once they got the card, the hospital was supposed to refund all the money I had given. However, the hospital refused on the grounds that they were asked to source supplies from outside for 'better quality'. I was still okay with it as I knew that she would get full care and I didn't have to spend more money.

Eighteen months later, Thanga was back on her feet

and started helping with the small kitchen garden at our cottage, and we would see her pleasant and content face at least twice a week. She recovered from a major operation and several rounds of chemotherapy, which reduced her to bones wrapped in thin skin. But during these eighteen months, she saw her son get married and got a grandson to keep her even happier.

15. Let children learn lasting lessons from nature around you

Nature and the wildlife around you can leave a much deeper impression on children than what they learn from you or at school. Our children are growing up watching a lot of wildlife around us; birds making nests, trying to teach their chicks to fly and protecting them from other predatory birds. Pied kingfishers take aim mid-flight and dive to catch fish whereas the blue kingfishers wait on a branch for fish to get closer and then dive. They see the seasonal changes, the arrival of the monsoon, and the arrival and departure of migratory birds. They get to see the different ways of fishing and how some fishermen use the forces of nature to their advantage to catch more fish with less effort.

I always find it better to use an analogy from nature if have to reinforce a point. For example, my second daughter picked up a bad habit while in England. When she was small, her nanny would insist on getting the plate back quickly so that she could wash it, put it away and get back to the sofa in front of the TV. My daughter would stuff the last few bites of food in her mouth to empty the plate and then chew them gradually. When we found out, we tried to talk her out of it but failed for many years. One Sunday, I spotted a garden snake struggling in the river closer to our property. We could see a bulge in its body close to the head and it couldn't move. When my daughters came back from Sunday school, it was still lying there. We were not sure if the snake would survive as it was clearly struggling. After four hours, it somehow managed to swim away and I explained to my daughter that that's what can happen when someone bites off more than they can chew. From that point on, she never stuffed food in her mouth. That one event put a stop to a habit we couldn't correct with years of lecturing.

16. Take children to funerals, not just weddings

My hairdresser in the UK once told me: 'Immigrants must have a pet with a life expectancy much shorter than yours; else your kids won't know what to do if something happens to you.'

One thing I learned during my professional life in the US and the UK was that it is better to be a hairdresser than a dentist in those countries as everyone loves their hairdresser but hates the dentist. I think it boils down to whom you can chat with the most.

My hairdresser in the UK was chatting with the customer before me about his dog. When it was my turn, she asked me, 'James, which pet do you have?' I told her that I didn't have a pet. She was astonished and said, 'You are a new immigrant with kids and you don't have a pet?' I asked her, 'What is the correlation between pets and immigrants?' She explained to me that immigrants' children only get to know people of their parents' age or less and only see weddings and baptisms. If they were living in their native place, kids would see an equal number of funerals and accept death as a natural process. She then suggested that I get a pet goldfish, which has a short life and is easy to maintain, to teach my kids the cycle of life.

When I reflected on her comments, I realized that she had a valid point. I had grown up in a situation where I had memorized funeral songs. After moving back to my home town, I made it a point to attend funerals of my relatives, even distant ones, and ensured that my kids attended them too.

With several ageing elderly relatives, we have an equal number of weddings, baptisms and funerals in a year. Instead of watching the goldfish die, they saw my godfather—my maternal uncle whose name I carry—go from someone who would collect delicious fruits for them from his farm one year to someone in a wheelchair with Alzheimer's the next. He eventually died in the hospital in the third year. My kids have now accepted death as a normal thing to be expected when people get older. My youngest one even started to extrapolate and once asked an uncle of mine, 'When are you going to die?' Now we caution her in advance!

RECHARGE

Most professionals rely on occasional expensive vacations to recharge their energy levels. Most HR theories talk about the work-life balance, which is a about making compromises to ensure that you don't try to reach your full potential at work by ruining your life or vice versa. What I experienced at God's Own Office was not work-life balance, it was work-life resonance. Both work and life vibrated at their natural frequencies and the resulting energy was bigger than the sum of both.

A frequent question I was asked about working from a village: 'Won't you get bored after some time if you move from the hustle and bustle of city life to a sleepy village?' My response: 'Not if you proactively fill your time with the activities which give you a lot of positive energy to recharge your mind and body.' Here are a few activities I recommend to make sure you not only avoid getting bored, but make life more exciting.

17. Adopt a farm for your kids and the farmer's life

'Dad, this is the most delicious jackfruit I have ever

eaten. What's even better is that we know where the tree is! We can eat this every year, hooray!'

My eldest daughter had just tasted the jackfruit we brought from the family farm. Her comment made me realize the difference between buying something from a shop, which we did for two years in Bangalore when each jackfruit tasted different, and getting it from the source. Her comments and perception, along with the conversations and insights from my professional world, led me to the conviction that I needed to adopt a farm for my kids.

A retired chief technology officer of Chevron was travelling around India with me to conduct a series of workshops for my top clients during my Microsoft stint. During this trip, Alan and his wife, Mary, shared their passion to reduce the carbon footprint. They had started farming with a goal to produce 40 per cent of what their family needed from their own garden in California. Secondly, my brother, based in Las Vegas, gave me a bottle of wine which read 'Moolakaat Wines', which is my family name. I got curious and he explained how his family spent several weekends at a winery to prepare the wine of their taste. I responded: 'If I put the value of your time, this is going to be the most expensive wine I will ever drink.' He quickly corrected me by saying that he would have spent more money to keep the kids busy during those weekends and, more importantly, now the whole family knows how wine is made.

I live in a place where the weather allows anything to grow and I was doing nothing to bring down my carbon footprint or to help my children learn how food gets to their plates. So, I partnered with a farm near my house. Now we take part in farming activities three to four times during each crop season and source organic produce from there.

Even professionals living in metros should consider adopting a farm within sixty to ninety minutes from your city, at least during your children's formative years. Modern farm equipment is comparable to the lawnmowers we happily operate when we lived abroad. Your children benefit significantly from the experience and, in the process, you motivate the farmer and provide him additional income by buying his produce directly without the middlemen.

18. Embrace local culture

Our policy is to treat all religious events as a deep cultural experience. This approach helps us appreciate and respect other religious events, some of which are really spectacular.

I have done photo features on many cultural and sporting events such as the Nehru trophy boat race at Alleppey, a once-in-twelve-years special ritual at Vaikom Siva temple wherein they draw a large three-dimensional *kalam* of the Devi with sixty-four hands known as the Vadakkupurathu pattu, etc. For four years, I have captured the Aluva Shivaratri, from the time they start building the temporary bridge across the river to when they dismantle it after the month-long festival. I block my calendar well in advance to participate in such spectacular events held nearby each year. The famous *Thrissurpooram* and *Chettikkulangara bharani* are still on my to-do list.

I attend the festivals at our local temple and watch evening theatre performances whenever possible. It is a pleasure to sit under a banyan tree and watch various traditional classical performances from Kathakali to

Mohiniyattam, and the arangettams at our local dance school where my daughters study. Ayyappavilakku, a major event at the temple, is very close to my daughter's birthday and we sponsor the cost of payasam for everyone at the temple that day. On my way back, I get a pot full of payasam for the birthday dinner. We also plan our holidays in a way that we attend major cultural programs like the annual arangettam at Kerala Kalamandalam or the annual dance and music festival at Tanjavur.

Finally, if you get your location right, you can have a constant source of energy from Mother Nature around God's Own Office. Just keep the tripod and the SLR ready to capture the wonderful moments while your colleagues are locked in their cubicle or stuck in traffic. All these gave me the energy and incentive to work extra hard to hold on to my work-life resonance. I always considered it a privilege to work from my home town and took the onus on myself to ensure that I was able to work as much, if not more, than I used to at the city offices.

DARK SIDE

19. Emotional fortitude to stomach avoidable deaths around you

By getting involved in the lives of poor people in Bharat, you also expose yourself to a lot of avoidable deaths, which you may not have to face in cities. This is the dark side of my life in Bharat, and one must be prepared to stomach it.

For two-and-a-half years, we had been involved with Thanga and her family to help her beat cancer. One day, I had agreed to drive Thanga and Moothakarumban to the medical college as her surgeon refused to treat the complications arising out of her second operation. We had thought her case was fully sorted as she got insurance from the state and additional funding from the state government lottery scheme. So, since money was not an issue and she had recovered well from the first operation, we took our eyes off the case.

To our utter disappointment, she ended up in palliative care a few weeks after the second operation, and nobody had any clue what happened.

One version is that her son's politician friends tried to demonstrate their ability to help the poor by getting a senior politician to call the surgeon. The politician apparently threatened the surgeon with dire consequences if Thanga was not given a private room as she had 'insurance'. But this backfired and the surgeon refused to see her ever again. I blame both her son and friends, who had accepted the fate that she would die two years ago because of lack of funds, till we intervened. I also blame the surgeon who took out his anger on a poor patient over the actions of a bunch of misguided youth.

Moothakarumban was clueless about what to do. He refused to file a complaint against the surgeon with the human rights commission since, according to him, 'doctors and nurses are like gods to us'. Thanga preferred to die than go through the ordeal, and the entire neighbourhood had reconciled to that fate. I cleared four hours between dropping off and picking up my kids from their summer classes to take Thanga to the medical college. Unfortunately, when I reached their home, Moothakarumban said, 'Sir, we can't go today, someone from the neighbourhood died yesterday.' A relative about the same age as Thanga's son was killed in a gang fight. The young man, who was already involved in several criminal cases, was beaten to death by a gang of six in broad daylight.

I was in Mumbai to host a roundtable with two authors from the Bay Area, one of whom I had met a day before I started my journey back home from the US via the UK. It was a very happy occasion for me as I was meeting the business leaders from Mumbai after a six-month break from the big ponds. I was very keen to see their reaction to my new avatar and to the rather comical business card that I had got printed just that weekend. I had a tough time letting go my elegant Circle of Excellence Platinum Club business card from Microsoft, especially printed from Redmond, that I had carried proudly for over four years. A few minutes into the meeting, I got a call from my small pond. It was Thanga's son. I couldn't take the call as I was running the show and continued with the meeting, but I knew something was wrong.

A week after the failed attempt to take Thanga to the medical college, I went to check on her again. I was a bit upset with Moothakarumban for delaying it and I told him somewhat harshly: 'If you get her help soon, she may be with you for another ten years. Otherwise you may lose her pretty soon.' He had promised to take her the very next day. And he did, first to the medical college and then to another doctor. When I first stopped in front of their house, there were more people than usual there. Moothakarumban came out of the house and followed my car to my cottage. As soon as I got down, he began telling me how the birds were eating my fruits. I was least bothered about the fruits and was keen to know about Thanga.

The doctor at the medical college had tried to reach the surgeon to find out what happened, but the surgeon was on a long leave. According to Moothakarumban, the doctor managed to contact the surgeon through 'Internet'. I assumed it must have been via email. The next day, he was told her cancer was very advanced and nothing could be done to save her, so it would be better to take her home and give her as much comfort as possible. Moothakarumban had taken her to one more hospital and got the same response. I was shocked, and just said, 'My god, this has gone out of our hands. We should have intervened before she was discharged after the second operation. The discharge sheet clearly says that the patient left against medical advice, so the surgeon will blame everything on you.' My words touched him and the old man's emotions burst like a dam. He broke down in front of me; I can't remember the last time I saw an adult crying that loudly. He said, 'Sir, the only mistake we made was asking for a room and for that, the surgeon stopped treating my wife. All our life, we both prayed at the temple as well as to our branthan muthappan at St Thomas mount church in Malayatoor. He won't escape punishment from both gods. His only son, a medical student, committed suicide a month after the second operation and more misfortune is going to come to him.' I consoled him and told him not to curse anyone and focus on his wife and leave the rest to god.

When you live in a small town, the stories are intertwined and the characters reappear in various parts of your life. A few months ago, I went to drop my wife at the medical college where she started working after the five-year break. We saw a picture of a young boy with a garland at the college gate. Later, my wife told me that was a first-year student, the only son of two doctors, who had committed suicide. I realized that the boy's father was Thanga's surgeon. I only know one version of Thanga's case from Moothakarumban, so I won't cast any judgment on anyone, but this coincidence was a bit too eerie to me.

Later, I went to see Thanga, who was in severe pain. But as soon as she saw me, she started smiling and enquired about my kids. I didn't stay long and told her that we would pray for her. The next week, she was admitted to the palliative care centre. I had gone to town to get my new business card from the local printer. There was a power outage at the press and the hospital was within walking distance, so I used the time to see Thanga. Her whole family was there. She again smiled and asked about my kids and wife. Moothakarumban, for the first time, said something to me in English: 'Tomorrow eight.' I didn't understand, so when I came out I asked his son, 'What was your dad trying to say about tomorrow eight?'

Apparently, Thanga was surviving on IV fluids and painkillers. The moment they stopped the medication, she would lose all her energy and her senses. The doctor was of the opinion that it was best to let her die than keep her alive artificially, and the decision would be taken at 8 a.m. tomorrow. Under medication and IV fluids, she was fully coherent and wasn't feeling the pain. So I suggested that they continue to keep her on IV fluids and all the family members should get back to normal work, and come to meet her every evening. Later, my wife told me that Thanga would not last more than few days with IV fluids, the pain would only get worse and it was best to go with the doctor's advice. I was supposed to call them to inform this, but I didn't have the emotional fortitude to pass on such a message.

My meeting in Mumbai went off well and as soon as the group left, I called Thanga's son and heard that she had passed away that morning. Eighteen months ago, I had made a similar call to him after my roundtable with Tom Friedman and I had received great news: the life of the rare turtle in my well was safe. Two authors, two meetings, two phone calls from the same person but my emotional pendulum swung to opposite ends. I told him that I wouldn't be back till Friday and they should proceed with the cremation. Though I was sad, the professional in me had to move on to three more meetings in Mumbai. Then I had to travel to Bangalore for the next roundtable in two days where the chefs at the hotel would prepare a range of Western dishes from the jackfruit Moothakarumban had plucked from the tree in my small farm.

I don't know enough details about what happened with Thanga's second operation, but I strongly feel that everyone around her, including me, could have done more to extend her life.

20. Mind the gap . . . bureaucracy in India

When we made the decision to move back to India and to our home town, we overlooked one major factor related to my wife's profession, which proved to be the most painful part of our journey home. If you or your spouse is a licensed professional, you must triple check all regulatory requirements in India.

Since my wife is a doctor, a highly regulated profession in any country, she had to take re-certification exams in the US and the UK to get the licence to practice. In 1999, when she was considering marrying me, she had written to the Medical Council of India (MCI), the licensing authority for doctors, asking whether her degree was recognized here. They swiftly wrote back to her, thanking her for her interest in working in India and saying that the degree was recognized in India as per a Medical Act and a particular schedule.

A few months after our third daughter was born, I made a trip to the Medical Council of India during a business trip to Delhi. I had the letter and my wife's certificates with me. I had to find out the formalities required to register her in India, so she could start practicing. I had no clue that the building, which resembles the Red Fort, would become a pilgrimage spot I had to visit every time I travelled to Delhi for many years. I got a real taste of bureaucracy in India, which I had forgotten during the decade I spent away. I was sent from pillar to post, made to wait at every stage and finally, I got to an officer who was the first in a chain of officers in charge of scrutinizing all international medical degrees. He was like a visa official trying to dismiss everyone who came his way. He looked at my papers and said, 'Your wife cannot work in India.'

I showed him the letter from 1999. He went through the letter and showed me a fine print, which my wife had overlooked. The degree is recognized by the Medical Act as per schedule so and so . . . if held by an Indian national. Doctors are the most sought after professionals all over the world and there are established procedures in almost all countries to get a doctor trained abroad to practice in their country.

Hence, you find Indian doctors in almost every country. However, in India it's one-way traffic. The largest exporter of doctors doesn't allow foreign nationals to practice in India unless it is for a charitable purpose or to train doctors in India.

My wife had the Overseas Citizen of India card, which gives her all rights of a citizen, except the power to vote. I told him that she had a full work permit, so should be treated as a national for the purpose of any work in India. I also offered to try and get a letter from the overseas affairs ministry, if that would help. He got a bit ticked off and said, 'Sir, we don't take instructions from any ministry. We are an independent regulator constituted by an act in Parliament in the 1960s and only another act by the Parliament can allow your wife to work in India.' He then asked me to leave. My only hope now was a new act in the Parliament, which I thought would happen for two reasons. India has one of the worst doctor to citizen ratio as per WHO standards. Secondly, there is a constant flow of foreign nationals moving to India to support the economic growth in the country, and some of their partners are going to be doctors.

Later I met one of the insurance industry veterans at

a conference in Khajuraho. He was in charge of drafting the new insurance act for India. He told me not to have too high hopes on a new medical act to solve my wife's issue. He had already spent two years in drafting the new Insurance Act and still had no visibility when it would be passed.

I was disheartened. The only options left were to either go back to the UK or change her nationality to Indian, for which she would qualify only after completing five years in India. We reconciled to the wait, but kept renewing her licence in the UK as we had lost trust in the system here. She managed to find a postgraduate diploma course for two years, which would help her to stay connected with medicine and understand diseases specific to India. MCI gave her permission to take the course, as they usually do for a lot of foreign students, who are a major source of income for medical colleges in India.

A year later, I received a flurry of emails from my senior colleagues at work about an announcement by the prime minister. India would allow foreign nationals with OCI card to get the licence to practice regulated professions like medicine. Six months later, the overseas affairs ministry issued an ordinance saying that all

OCI card holders should be treated as Indian nationals for the purpose of professional licence registrations. I quickly headed back to the MCI with a copy of the ordinance to prove that my wife was now on a par with Indian nationals, so she should get the licence as per the letter they gave her in 1999. Again, I was sent from pillar to post as nobody wanted to take a decision in our case. Finally, I was sent to the lawyers representing the MCI at the Supreme Court. Everyone promised there might be a way out, but wouldn't give me an official reply. By that time, my trips to the MCI had got branded as a licence-hunting activity among my colleagues at Microsoft.

After another year of hunting, a member of the staff found a reason why they couldn't give my wife the licence. He used a Supreme Court ruling and said, 'Even though we had accepted that your wife's degree is recognized in 1999, she didn't officially apply for registration at that time. As per the new Supreme Court ruling, all new applicants need to pass a qualification exam to register. But another ruling says that only those who graduated after 2004 are required to take the test, so we can't make a decision in your wife's case as she graduated in 2000.' I couldn't be more frustrated.

Either they should have said she was eligible for the registration, or that she needed to take the test to get the registration rather than wait for another Supreme Court instruction. But they kept her case in limbo yet again.

One thing I noticed over the years was that when the Parliament sessions were on, the last flight from Delhi to Kochi on Friday nights always had cabinet ministers from Kerala. I made a last-minute decision to upgrade my flight to business class to get access to the ministers and to try my luck with them. The cabinet minister for overseas affairs was sitting right in front of me and the person behind me was the father of a speaker at one of my events. I had met the elderly man when I went to their house to brief his son about the event. But the biggest surprise was that one of the board members of MCI was returning to Kerala, and sitting right next to me. I had seen him at MCI but never had a chance to meet him. The old man introduced me to the minister and, before I even reached out to the minister, the board member reviewed my application. He said that our case was never presented to the board, and he found my wife's case to be one of the most legitimate ones he had come across. He agreed to have a word with the new secretary and do whatever was legally possible. It took another six months for my wife to get a letter saying that she needed to take the test. Then another six months to get the licence.

The first principle I learned about supply chain at Warwick was that 'throughput of the whole supply chain will always be the throughput of the worst bottle neck in the supply chain'. And the first principle I learned from this experience is 'the throughput of any top bureaucrat in India will always be the throughput of their worst performing staff'. Hence, please do not underestimate the time and effort required if you have to deal with bureaucracy in India. On the positive side, it's possible to hold on to your values and ethics and still get things done if you do not try to take shortcuts. There are still a lot of upright officials who can help you out.

For the past one year, my wife has been working at a mission hospital near us.

21. Lots of humility, patience and tolerance

When you live in a small town, you interact with fewer people than you would in the city, but you meet them again and again in several walks of your life. Your children's schoolteacher could be attending the same church as yours and the shop you frequent could be owned by their classmate's dad. The postman or the telephone guy could be living close to your place. The best experience for me was when my daughter came back and said, 'Dad, my Sunday school teacher told me she taught you when you were small.'

When all is going well in the small pond, it is very idyllic. The flipside is that if you start having problems with people in a small town, they don't go away, and start reappearing everywhere you go. If you are not careful, it is very easy to get into conflicts, mostly ego clashes, with people around you. First of all, you were away for a long time and then reappeared in the scene, attracting some importance. Most people will be happy to see you back, and you can win their goodwill by treating them with respect, getting involved in helping them and participating in local festivals. But some may think of you as a threat for various silly reasons.

For three years, we had a pleasant experience and we integrated well into the neighbourhood. One morning, we woke up to a group of people shouting slogans and vandalizing the beautiful garden in the back of our property near the river. I had taken lead in convincing other owners in our apartment to clean and beautify the area. We have one of the best varieties of mango growing by the river and children like to pick up ripe mangoes from the ground during summer. Since I had spotted many snakes by the river, we had to first clear the overgrown wild creepers and grass between the river and the retainer wall. While clearing the creepers, we spotted old steps of a bathing ghat to the river. There used to be an ancient courtyard house on the property, and it must have been their bathing ghat, which fell into ruin by years of neglect.

We asked the local panchayat representatives if we could clear the mud deposited by the ghat and keep it as a spot to feed bread to fish. In addition, we offered to clean the panchayat-owned bathing ghat for women near us. They supported the idea and, in addition, the local women were very happy to get their bathing ghat cleaned. In the next three days, we got everything cleaned up. One resident brought orchids from her house and planted them on poles around the garden. Within days, the group vandalized the whole garden, broke all orchid plants and drove bikes through the lawn, destroying it completely.

The leader of the group was someone I had met
many times at the temple. He had even given me a pot of
payasam once after a festival. He claimed orchids were
not native to the region, were not environment-friendly
and we had no right to beautify the land by the river.
A part of the land belongs to the government, which
is the case with all properties by rivers in Kerala. But
those living by the river have the full right to use the
land till the government comes up with a project. His
comment on orchids not being environment-friendly
ticked me off and I wanted to show him the wild
orchid from Mahabharata on one of the trees near us.
He then printed and placed more flex boards than the
number of orchids he destroyed through the streets,
causing more damage to the environment and making
it unsafe to drive.

Most members from the apartment complex wanted
to file a police case against the group and its leader. But
some of us were able to persuade them to be patient
and try to win the group over. That would provide
permanent relief than having a defeated neighbour
waiting for the next battle to win. He wanted us to close
the cleared bathing ghat, which we agreed to, but the
very next day a pair of kingfishers started building their

nest there and he had to back off. He would send kids to play football in the area to disturb us, but they gave up after a few days. The ball would end up in the river every third kick, and we had to ask our security staff to keep an eye on them because of the risk of drowning or being bitten by a snake. Later, some of his friends started using that area for playing cards and consuming alcohol. But the cops spotted them one day and many of them ended up in the police station.

It has been two years since the incident; the group leader gave up instigating people as most of them realized we had only good intentions. The public bathing ghat for women is back to being full of weeds. He works for one of my local service providers and I see him every time I go there to make a payment. He used to avoid eye contact, but has started smiling again.

Once, the principal of my daughter's school called me to her office and gave me a piece of her mind as we had missed one of the many circulars related to the school reopening. If it was in the city, I would have accepted my fault and given her constructive feedback to give all circulars at once on the day we came to meet her teacher. Instead, I just accepted my fault, apologized, came back and created a file folder in my office cabinet for circulars till she graduated to the next school. I had seen my short-tempered dad and my brothers showing extreme humility when they met my teachers when I was at school, so I didn't forget that teachers are used to that in small towns. At the end of the year, I was invited to speak at the graduation ceremony to thank all the teachers on behalf of the parents.

THE ECONOMICS

22. The economics of God's Own Office

Many colleagues have asked me how I afford to live in my home town and spend a week at my office in Bangalore at my own expense. They assume that the cost of accommodation and transportation in Bangalore and the flight tickets must eat into my salary. Many even suggested that I should ask the company to pay for those expenses, which I was dead set against as a future manager could look at my model as an extra burden on his or her travel and expenses budget. My colleagues have seen me fly down just for a customer dinner or to attend a golf practice session organized by a partner for some of our top customers. Before we discuss how I managed those expenses, let's first compare the cost of living in a metro versus that in a small town in India, based on my experience of having stayed in Bangalore for eighteen months after we first landed in India.

a. Housing cost in Aluva, where we live, is a third of what we used to pay in Bangalore for the same space. Here, however, the quality of accommodation and location is much better.

b. School fees for children are also significantly lower. The quarterly fee we used to pay at the international schools in Bangalore is the same as what we pay for the whole year here at the convent school meant for children of all economic backgrounds.

c. Unlike in Bangalore, there is no need for a driver in Aluva since it's a small town and I work from home. In Bangalore, we needed a driver as my office was an hour away and the car had to be brought back for my wife.

d. In Aluva, we also end up paying less for fuel for the same reason.

e. I used to buy lunch every day at work in Bangalore.

Now, I eat home-cooked food made from fresh organic vegetables and fish bought from our neighbourhood at a fraction of the cost.

f. Holiday costs have also come down significantly as we used to travel many times a year from the city to our home town to visit relatives or attend family functions on a short notice.

Overall, we have at least a 30 per cent reduction in the cost of living every year. The difference in housing cost alone is more than the cost of flying to Bangalore and staying there for a week every month. In addition, I would save up all my reward points from my credit card and the air miles with the airline which had the most convenient flights between Kochi and Bangalore. Hence, I got most of my tickets to Bangalore at a much cheaper cost.

So, at God's Own Office, you can easily afford to be penny foolish and pound wise when it comes to flying down just for a dinner or a golf game. In addition, you can build a fund for your future start-up or for a sabbatical to work on your passion, both of which I am doing.

23. Offer small donations, decline loan requests

When you live in a small town, you are bound to come across people with temporary financial difficulties. You could get a lot of requests for short-term loans, which you may be able to afford. But this is a real danger and one should be conscious of the wider risk involved. I learned it the hard way. An acquaintance was in a difficult financial situation and it appeared that his business would stop if he didn't make one payment. The main investor for his business is a well-respected industrialist from Kerala, whom I knew very well. I felt obliged to help him out as he was trying his best to start something on his own in an industry with stiff competition from players with decades of experience.

I was still a bit nervous. I checked with a few business contacts and asked if I was getting a promissory note and a post-dated cheque from someone whom I could count on. My friend was offering those thing, so I went ahead, but it turned out to be a disheartening experience. For the first time, I received a letter from my bank that one of my cheques had bounced. It was the post-dated cheque he had given with the promissory note from his CFO. It has been two years and I still haven't got half the money he borrowed for two months. More than the money, it ruined my appetite to help anyone in such situations and to trust even people I know. A lot of people are in this situation in small towns due to the unpredictability of payments from their customers. They end up borrowing money from whoever they can find. Over time, they start borrowing from one to repay whoever is shouting the most, and you can't win the shouting game with career money lenders.

From that experience, I adopted a policy which has worked well for me. Prioritize start-ups that find your experience and industry contacts more valuable than the small sums of money they can borrow from you. I make it clear that the day I feel like investing in their firm, I will stop being a mentor and start assessing their actions as an investor instead. A mentor's job is to help the mentees even if they are not the best. An investor should focus on their investment returns, critically evaluate every action and only pick the best from the pack.

In case you want to help an entrepreneur financially,

buy their products or services at a higher rate than the market price and even give them a cash advance. This will also help you to evaluate them as a customer and then recommend them to others. Or, ask them to take a loan from the bank and donate the interest amount if you can afford it. The bank will do the chasing and the shouting.

Requests for financial aid from people from poor backgrounds are mostly on health grounds or for their children's education. If you get involved, you will realize that they can avail many government schemes and if they can't, it's better to donate than lend money to them. Otherwise, they will start avoiding you from to the guilt of not being able to pay back as promised, and you end up losing both the money and their services.

24. Beware: Missing a flight could be very costly

Connections between metros and small towns are predictable, especially the last flight of the day. The last flight from New Delhi is taken by a lot of politicians and ministers from Kerala. The last flights from

Mumbai and other metros are taken by industrialists from Kerala and are used as connecting flight by several international passengers to Kerala. So, I never had an issue of flight cancellations as the airlines pay extra attention to the last flights, which are usually full. But, I had to treat the last flights like an international flight and always reached the airport on time as missing that flight would cost me dearly. But the situation is very different when you are flying between two small towns in India, where you have to use a connecting flight via a metro. Then you are at the mercy of the flight from a small town to reach the metro in time to make the connection. Even if you plan a sufficient gap, it is quite unpredictable. Though I rarely travelled between small towns, I still had several nail-biting moments.

Once, after organizing a conference in Khajuraho, three delegates and I decided to get up early for a safari tour of Panna National Park and the Pandava falls.

When we got back to the hotel after our trip, we had bad news waiting for us. Khajuraho was covered by fog, so no flights were landing or taking off and our return was delayed. The keynote speaker saw the stress on my face and approached me. He said, 'Son, don't blame yourself for this delay. You had planned everything well, now the matter is between us and the airlines.' I replied, 'No, sir, I wasn't worried about that. Tomorrow is my daughter's first birthday and we have invited a lot of people for the party. I will be in a soup if I don't get back tonight.' He said, 'Don't worry, unpredictability is part of India and you need a backup plan for everything. That's how I managed for the last fifty years. Find out how many people are desperate to get to Delhi tonight and go by road.' Reluctantly, some of us booked a car. Fortunately the fog cleared in the afternoon and we were able to take the flight. I made it in time for my daughter's birthday.

In my opinion, don't plan anything important the day after your return if you are flying back from a small town. Book connections with the same airline, so in case you have to stay back, it will be at their expense.

25. Consider the value of time at the time of moving

We have moved as a family across continents several times and the one thing I have learned is that the time you spend searching for stuff to buy is more expensive than the cost of moving your possessions, even if you use professional movers. You want to hit the ground running as soon as possible. Consider the amount of time and arguments you would have had choosing a painting, a couch or even stuff for the kitchen. When we moved from the US to the UK, we had to give away most electronic stuff due to the voltage difference between the two countries. We also got rid of all our furniture as it was too big to fit through doors in the UK and it would have been expensive to ship it. Since we were shipping our car, we managed to keep all kitchen items, linen and our daughter's toys in it. When the car arrived in the UK, it was a huge relief, almost like getting a part of our life back, especially for our daughter. Children feel very insecure when you move around, but if you are able bring a part of their life like furniture, toys, plates, cups, etc., it gives them some amount of comfort.

Back in the UK, we ended up spending more time selecting furniture even though we had half as much time on our hands then since we were both working and had to take care of a child. Later, when we moved from the UK to India, we brought everything possible with us, including furniture. I got movers to set up the rooms exactly like we had in the UK. We still use the furniture. It may not look new, but it saved us a lot of time and our kids found it comforting. I may still have a piece of junk I had in my attic in the UK sitting in one of the overhead storage units of the same room! You will find a way to repurpose the stuff in your new place. For example, my wife and I spent several days looking for a matching wooden coat hanger for our wooden flooring. It is now being used in the kitchen balcony to hang banana bunches while we wait for them to turn ripe. The electric barbeque hot plate I had as a backup in case of rain in the UK is now being used to make dosas when we have guests over. The telescopic branch pruner I used to cut tree branches in the UK is now being used to cut jackfruits from tall trees.

Whenever you move your home and home office in a village, keep at least a month as a buffer. Make sure you have everything working at the new place before you let go of the current one. As usual in India, our builder overshot his deadline by a year. We had to stay in a rented place for the first year to make sure our kids started school at the beginning of the academic year. When it was time to move in, the builder confirmed that everything was in working condition and I could move in and start working from there. To play it safe, I kept the rented place for two more months and moved everything except my office-related stuff. There was disaster waiting for us. We were the first ones to move in, and within a week, almost all electrical equipment was knocked out from a power surge and we had to get everything repaired. Since I had kept the office at the old place, I could still work from there without interruption and moved it a month later when everything was stable at the new place.

26. Though you live in a village, you need to appear like you're from the metro

Though my dress code at God's Own Office is shorts and a T-shirt, for eight to ten days a month I needed to operate like a professional from the city. One morning, during the first monsoon after we moved back, I opened the cupboard to pick up my business suit for a trip. To my shock, it was covered in a layer of fungus. This was at the rented accommodation where we first stayed. The wall behind the built-in cupboard was exposed to the rain and the humidity. I had to make that trip with a sports jacket and as soon as I got back, I bought a readymade cupboard which can be kept away from the wall. That resolved the issue.

The next challenge I had was to find a reliable dry-cleaner. I had already had a bad experience in Bangalore, when our driver took my best suit to a local dry-cleaner and it came back shrunk. Initially, I got dry-cleaning done at the hotels where I stayed for meetings, but that was not a permanent solution. I got the solution from the hotel near the airport, which is my backup office as well as the place where I meet contacts who visit from cities. I asked for their dry-cleaner and the factory turned out to be close to where we live. I went there one day and discussed with the owner if he would dry clean my clothes if I dropped them off at the factory. The factory works round-the-clock hours and for the past five years, I have been getting express, five-star quality service from this place at a much cheaper rate. The dry-cleaning factory then led me to the best linen shop in town and that led me to the best tailor in town. Over time, I switched to linen completely, which helps me fit in well in the corporate world and government circles in the metros. The best part is that selecting clothes is now down to just two variables—colour and thread count—and I can have the exact same fit ready in two weeks.

FIVE

A MONDAY AT GOD'S OWN OFFICE

At 6 a.m., I wake up to the sound of thousands of egrets flying off from the trees across the river. I then go to my home office with my supersized cup of morning tea. One good thing about working early in the morning in India is that your colleagues from the US headquarters are still online. Most senior executives in India also tend to work early in the morning. I first scan my mail to see if there's anything important. If my colleagues are online, I chat with them or speak to them from my laptop. I continue to work till 8 a.m. If any decisions are required from senior executives, I get them over email before their day gets packed with meetings. I also close many issues with my international colleagues before they go to sleep.

By this time, my kids get ready to go to school and at 8 a.m., I take them to the bus stop and proceed for my morning walk. On most days, I cross the railway track, walk by the paddy fields towards the river, 500 metres from where we live. The first stop is usually at Sivan's fresh fish shop on the river bank. Every morning, fishermen bring their catch to Sivan's shop and if I like anything, he brings it to my flat by the time I return from my walk. Some of the fish are still alive by the time he gets there. Then I take the footpath on the railway bridge across the river. There are two tracks and at least one train goes past by the time I cross the bridge. The sound of fast trains on the bridge and the shock absorbers between two cabins takes me back to my automotive days, when I used to watch heavy-duty metallic presses cut and shape thick metal sheets into parts of a car. After crossing the bridge, I get on to the main Palace road in our small town and walk down another 500 metres. During this stretch, I normally spot the school bus with my kids on board. The bus travels 6 km to reach the spot as it has to cross two bridges and pick up other kids on the way.

My kids and their friends wave at me, while the driver and the staff still don't understand where I rush to in the morning. They see that I'm absolutely fine when I drop the kids but by the time they find me on Palace road, I am completely drenched in sweat. In a village, most people sweat at work or when they are late for something, so they can't understand my concept of forcing myself to sweat. I then take a break at a ferry landing spot next to Aluva Palace and diagonally across the river from where I live. I stand under a mango tree from where I can see the morning activities at the Siva temple across the river, with my flat behind the temple as a backdrop.

This is my time to sync with many mentors I have from the corporate world. I am quite lucky to have some current and former chiefs of major corporations as mentors. And the best time to call this category of mentors is between 8.30 and 8.45 a.m. They are ready for the day but haven't started their busy meetings yet. The calls are usually short as I am looking for specific advice on a decision I need to make. It could be to check if a particular speaker or experience will appeal to people of their profile or it could be advice on a career decision. Considering the depth of the experience they have, they only need seconds to assess my situation and recommend the best option. Over time, our municipal corporation added a noisy engine to the ferry service, which made it difficult for me to make any phone calls from there. I found another, quieter, spot just fifty metres before the Palace. This one is also under a mango tree by the river, but many decades older. This spot was near the Advaita Ashram of Sree Narayana Guru, a famous guru from Kerala who fought against the caste system and preached the concept of one caste, one religion and one god for mankind. I feel a lot of positive energy at that spot. I can see fish jump in the water and, occasionally, a few pilgrims walk down the steps from the ashram temple, pray, take a holy dip in the river and make an offerings for the souls of their loved ones. Later, one of the priests at my children's school told me why I felt so much positive energy at that spot. That's where Mahatma Gandhi, Rabindranath Tagore and Acharya Vinoba Bhave met Sree Narayana Guru. It is also the location of India's first conference of all religions. After that, I started calling it my morning sync-up point with gurus of the past and present, the latter being my mentors.

On the way back, in case my calls with my mentors

don't take long, I stop by at my adopted farm, an organic farm owned by the state government and managed by a very enterprising agricultural officer. The 15 acre farm is surrounded by the river on three sides and the railway track on the fourth, so it is literally cut off from everywhere, making it ideal for organic farming. The pet dogs on the farm meet me at the entrance and walk in front of me, which, I'm told by the workers, is a good thing as the dogs look out for snakes. I take a short walk around the farm to check out the paddy at various stages of development. I greet the workers who start early and see if there are any organic vegetables ready for us to buy that week. My uncles used to do this walk across our paddy field with me when I was a child.

Then I quickly get back home and, as I walk past our local temple, I meet the priest, who has just completed the morning prayers. We both chat on our way back; his house is two doors down from our flat. I take a shower, have my breakfast and get back to work by 9.30 or 9.45 a.m. That's when most people get to work in the metros after a frustrating sixty to ninety minute struggle through traffic. The rest of the day is like in any office—emails, conference calls, video conferences, presentations, etc.—except that my lunch is hot, home-cooked food, sometimes including fresh fish caught that morning. I continue to work till the egrets return to the trees near us around 7 p.m. I then spend time with my kids, who come back from school by 4 p.m. and go to play in the park downstairs. Most colleagues in the metros start their gruelling journey back home around that time.

This makes me more productive, 50 per cent of the time that I save in my commute is spent on work and 50 per cent on my health and spirit. On an average, I get fifteen days like these in a month.

Sometimes, I change my morning walk route to the opposite side from the river, by the irrigation canal near the little cottage we own. I see older children dressed in uniforms walking to school, and younger children playing in the canal while their mothers wash clothes. Occasionally, I spot turtles, mongooses and a lot of birds. Once I reach our cottage, I take whatever is ready at the small yard there that day—curry leaves, papaya, mangoes, jackfruit, bilimbi, kasava, coconut or bananas. During my kids' summer holidays or when we have guests staying with us, I work from the attic of this cottage to free up my office room for them.

A team working without borders or time at God's Own Office

One morning, at 6 a.m., Ravi Venkatesan sent a mail to the leadership team and me saying that Microsoft corporate CFO Chris Liddell had offered to pick Mumbai as one of the six cities in the world to host a CFO Forum with fellow CFOs in India. Ravi wanted to know our opinion. From an executive engagement point of view, the CIOs were giving me feedback that we needed to win the mindshare of their CFOs. I felt that the offer from Chris was a great opportunity and I was aware of the impact he made with the CFOs earlier in London. I quickly responded to Ravi, saying that this was a good opportunity and I would be happy to take ownership in executing this high-profile event, if everyone agreed. Rajan, the then MD, supported me and the decision was made within minutes, even before many on the mailing list got a chance to read the mail.

I started working on 'Operation CIO to CFO', which was a massive exercise which required our sales team to identify the most critical CFOs for our business for the next three years, my mentors and contacts in the industry to identify the right topics, and speakers who could appeal to CFOs in India as well as local and corporate marketing team and Liddell's office. Once a short list of speakers and attendees was completed, I managed to sign up an elite set of speakers for the CFO Forum—celebrities of the financial press and business channels—with the help of Liddell's office and Ravi. Once the agenda was secured, I started personally inviting the top 100 CFOs in India and the event turned out to be a huge success, with registrations closing within four weeks. This is the first time Microsoft India was trying to do an event for CFOs, and the entire leadership team was very excited to hear the great response that we got. This turned out to be good for the business as well, with one of the CIOs declaring, 'I am now ready to take a proposal to the CFO to standardize on Microsoft platform.' We received a mail saying Liddell was thrilled to see the great preparations India had made compared to the other countries.

The first bombshell came on 2 October, Gandhi Jayanti. While driving to church, my phone rang. I looked at the number and saw it was Hiren, the India CFO. Since he was calling on a national holiday I realized it must be urgent. As we reached the church I quickly checked my smartphone. Turns out Liddell would not be able to travel to India for the CFO Forum due to personal reasons, so he could either have one of his direct reports attend the meeting or we could postpone the event. Three weeks from the biggest event I had ever organized, and the star attraction and the primary host was pulling out. The leadership team wanted to know whether to postpone or go with a substitute. I recommended that we postpone, but also said that we needed a new date in twenty-four hours and I would come up with a communication plan to limit the fallout. I called back and first tried to persuade him and the rest of the leadership team to go back to Liddell. Explain how great the event was looking and that there couldn't be anything more important than this for him, professionally or personally, so he should reconsider his decision. I got some very candid advice from Hiren: 'My dear friend, this is how life is in the big league. A no at this level is a No. Let's pick up the pieces from here and move on. I agree with your recommendation and let's hope for the best.'

One good thing about being in India is that we are diagonally opposite the Pacific Coast in the US, with an almost twelve-hour difference. So, if you have a good partner in that time zone, you can work on a crisis like

171

this round the clock. You pass the baton when you go to sleep and pick it up when you wake up, though at times you feel like you never slept. That night, I got into action after my kids went to sleep. Connected with my partner for the CFO Forum, Gerry, we came up with a plan: we needed a new date and ideally for Liddell to personally write to all speakers about the change, requesting them to join him on the new date. By the time I woke up, Gerry would have the date and a communication plan in place. Then, while Gerry slept, I would have to re-secure the venue for the new date. I signed off at 11.30 p.m. after drafting a mail which Liddell would send to all the speakers and the next morning at 6.00 a.m., I was back talking to my computer, with Gerry on the other end. We had a new date in February, and Liddell had agreed to send a personal email not just to the speakers, but to all thirty-five CFOs who had agreed to attend. Gerry had already reached out to the speaker from MIT, who was okay with the new date. By 8 a.m., the Taj Mahal Palace hotel, which was still undergoing renovation after the Mumbai terror attack, reconfirmed the new date and I communicated the plan of action to the India leadership team, which gave me the go ahead. That night, an email went out to all speakers from Liddell, and next morning, between 8.30 a.m. and 9.30 a.m., during my morning walk, I spoke to all their secretaries. By 9.30 a.m., I hit bullseye—all speakers reconfirmed and we had the same agenda and venue with a new date.

I got back to work at 10 a.m. I drafted an email for the thirty-five attendees, with the catch phrase, 'However, all speakers have kindly agreed for the new date.' The next day, by 6.30 a.m. IST, Liddell sent the mail out to all thirty-five, and almost twenty of them responded within an hour with reconfirmation. That's what most successful executives do early morning—check their email! By 10 a.m., we had thirty reconfirmations and the event was back on track after seventy-two hours of round-the-clock teamwork with Gerry.

The second bombshell came three weeks before the rescheduled event. At 6 a.m., I read an email announcement from Steve Ballmer saying that Chris Liddell had resigned and the new CFO was Peter Klein. Six months' work would be for nothing unless I salvaged the situation within two hours, before my speakers and attendees read the news in India. Once they cancelled their appointments, it would take me at least three months to get a slot on their calendar.

Another rapid-fire collaboration with Gerry in the US and, within two hours, I managed to secure a confirmation from Klein that he would honour the commitment and travel to India in three weeks. It was probably the first appointment Klein confirmed, that too involving foreign travel, within hours after his appointment. At 8 a.m., I sent a mail to all the speakers with the update that Klein was the new CFO of Microsoft and would be hosting the India CFO Forum on the same date. By 9 a.m., I got a confirmation from all the secretaries. By 9.15 a.m., I sent a mail to the leadership and sales team saying that there would be no change to the CFO Forum and that Klein would host the session. All speakers had reconfirmed. Both the leadership team and the employees were pleasantly surprised, with one of them sending a mail to everyone saying that they are not used to such swift responses. It's not that difficult if you have the right discipline, right set of technology to collaborate instantly with employees around the world, and the comfort of God's Own Office.

We had a great engagement with the top CFOs of India for the first time and, as a reward, Ravi and Gerry secured a special approval for me to attend Microsoft's

Global CEO Summit, where Bill Gates and Steve Ballmer host the top 100 CEOs in the world for two days. Attending the summit as a fly on the wall, with the titans of the corporate world, was by far the most stimulating professional experience for me. Within eighteen hours, I switched back to being a small fish in my pond at God's Own Office.

SIX

I REST MY CASE

1. Why small towns in India should embrace God's Own Office

From my experience of moving back to Kerala and continuing my national role at Microsoft, I think that small towns in India are missing a huge opportunity to motivate more professionals to come back and work from here. States are chasing corporations to set up operations in their IT parks. However, corporations will go wherever they can get the best employees at the lowest possible cost. While states continue to chase big corporations, they should also make a greater effort to make it easier for professionals to work from their home towns. Though small towns cannot compete with the social infrastructure of the metros, if one looks at the characteristics of the current mid-level managers, there is a lot these towns can offer to attract them.

Most mid-level managers in the IT Industry are well-travelled and stay in India by personal choice. After a fast-paced career, they are focused on providing educational and cultural stability for their children. They are also environmentally conscious and concerned with the safety of their children in the cities.

Most small towns offer several benefits to attract these professionals. These include great internet connectivity, even in villages, and a network of IT parks away from traffic hotspots, which save at least ninety minutes every day. Luxury holidays are just a short drive away and one can adopt a farm to reduce one's carbon footprint as well as for the overall development of kids. The cost of living is also significantly lower compared to the metros.

IT companies have a concept of 'hot desk' for consultants and sales people, who are always travelling. Whenever they come to the office, they can sit at any of the open office spaces assigned as the 'hot desk', where they can connect their laptop, phone, etc. and use it as their office desk. My suggestion is that small towns should create such 'hot desk' spaces in IT parks, which professionals can pay to use when they visit home. To start with, many professionals will start utilizing these spaces during school vacations and, over time, they will start extending their stay in their home towns. Once they start tasting the benefits of working from their home towns for a short period, they will seek more time to work from there, leading to eventual relocation. This can also attract more tourism to small towns. During school holidays, the family can extend their stay, while one of the parents continues to work from the nearest 'hot desk' during the day.

NRIs only spend about 15 per cent of their income in their home towns, which is still a huge source of revenue for the states. If they work from their home town, they will spend 100 per cent of their income in the state, creating a lot more job opportunities. We will start seeing more advertisements focused on the whole family living in small towns instead of just ads for gold, wedding sarees, properties targeted towards NRIs and muesli power for the aged!

There is hope for all Indian professionals feeling stuck in the metros. The Indian government has announced a plan to build 100 smart cities linked by high-speed trains and low-cost airports. If this becomes a reality, there will be 100 more locations for states and city professionals to create God's Own Offices.

2. Why big corporations should embrace God's Own Office*

Let's be honest, nobody really craves working from home. Given a choice, we would all like to have a Chinese wall between our 'sweet home' and the 'hot seat' in our office. By working from home you become this weird person for your family who is there but not approachable, with your head constantly buried in the laptop and shouting at someone they can't see. In India, you have the additional headache of setting up multiple levels of backup for broadband, electricity, etc. at your home. The very low percentage of employees currently availing this option validates this point. So, who really works from home/remote location? There are three categories of people—the creative, the subject-

---

* Adapted from a column I wrote for *ET*.

matter experts and the unfortunate with a personal family situation.

The Creative: These are the kind of employees who need a lot of oxygen for their creative energy to flow; they will gravitate towards the best place where they can be most creative. The best example of this is the late Verghese Kurien of Amul Cooperative. When the Indian government offered him the plum post to head the National Dairy Development Board (NDDB) in Delhi, he refused. His main source of energy was the farmers of Anand in Gujarat and, eventually, the government moved the headquarters of NDDB to Anand to make India self-sufficient on milk.

The Subject-Matter Experts: Or The Artisans, as Tom Friedman and Michael Mandelbaum describe them in their book, *That Used to Be US*. These people possess a unique skill set or knowledge that they have acquired and refined over a long period of time. They worked really hard and sacrificed a lot of time away from family in the initial years to reach the artisan stage and now, every piece of work or project they do has a unique signature style, which no one else can replicate easily. They are highly sought after and everyone in need will reach out to them wherever they are. Hence, whenever possible, they would like to give back some time, otherwise wasted on the long commute to office, to their family.

The Unfortunate with a personal family situation: These personal situations could be an ailing parent, childcare needs or if a spouse/partner is temporarily posted in another location and their job cannot be done remotely, e.g. hospital/factory. I am not including strike actions by political parties or flash floods during monsoon, when there isn't any way you can reach office and employers plead with everyone to work from wherever they can.

By not encouraging employees to work remotely, you will lose the first two categories or you will make them just show up but won't get their 100 per cent, which is suicidal for any organization as they are far too critical for the business. The third category will be forced to make a choice between family and job, which is quite unfortunate as in most cases, the situation is only temporary.

Speed and collaboration

According to some managers, speed and quality are often compromised when employees work from home. On the contrary, speed is what you get when employees work from home. Most of us now wake up to the alarm on the smartphone and with another touch we check if there are any responses to the emails we sent the previous day. In case we find an urgent mail, those who can work from home will grab a coffee and start working right away. This kind of speed is very helpful, especially for organizations where the teams are spread across the globe in different time zones. A response at 7 a.m. from your home is fourteen hours faster for an employee in San Francisco than a response at 9 a.m. from your Bangalore office.

Unless your entire team is based in one office location, your online presence is more important than your physical presence in an office where only a fraction of your team is based. With the right set of technologies and discipline, employees can collaborate as effectively from their city office.

To employers: I completely agree that not all roles in an organization can effectively be performed from home and it is best to hold the employee's manager and skip-level manager accountable to make those decisions based on clear performance goals.

To employees: Working from home is a privilege and the onus is on you to ensure that you perform better than those working from office. After all, you save at least ninety minutes of commute every day. In addition, you should also make it a priority to participate in as many team-building activities and social occasions at work, even if you have to shell out some money from your pocket.

Thus, I rest my case for God's Own Office. To all Indian professionals wherever you are, COME HOME!

A CHECKLIST FOR GOD'S OWN OFFICE

1. Do you have an unwavering conviction to return home?

2. Do you have a constant focus to return home? Does that keep you awake?

3. Have you earned the right to return? Can you pass the Mohammed versus Mountain test?

4. Can you still uproot your family? Can you still pass the inchworm test?

5. Do you have the right location for God's Own Office?

    a. Easy travel connectivity to your base office

    b. Reliable digital connectivity

   c. Constant source of positive energy to work alone

6. Can you arrange enough backup to avoid disruptions?

   a. Power

   b. Broadband

7. Do you or your employer have the right technology for remote working?

   a. Digital presence information

   b. Instant messenger

   c. Online audio/video conferencing

   d. Desktop sharing

   e. Remote access to corporate network

   f. Cloud services to store and share data

8. Can you make your home office sound proof?

9. Do you have the discipline?

   a. Work without supervision

   b. Handle interruptions by family and guests

10. Can you still stay on top of the mind of your colleagues and management?

11. Can you be a local ambassador for your employer?

12. Do you have options to adopt start-ups near your home town?

13. Can you ensure the safety of your family when you are away from home?

14. Can you allocate sufficient time to help your children remain globally competent in a small town?

15. Can you help your children integrate well in a regular school?

16. Are you willing to help people around you?

17. Are you happy to reconnect with extended family back home?

18. Can you find enough activities to recharge yourself in a sleepy village?

    a. Adopt a farm

    b. Participate in cultural activities

19. Do you have the resilience to stomach the dark sides of a small town?

a. Avoidable deaths around you

b. Bureaucracy

c. Need for extra humility, patience and tolerance

20. Will the economics of God's Own Office work for you?

ACKNOWLEDGEMENTS

First and foremost, I would like to thank Ravi Venkatesan for being a guide and role model for me on many occasions. I would like to thank Microsoft for supporting my return to India and for allowing me to work from my God's Own Office so that I could realize my full potential as a professional.

I would also like to acknowledge Anil Dharker and Thomas Friedman for injecting the power of writing into my head during the Mumbai Literature Live 2011, and the organizers of the Chennai Hindu Lit for Life for introducing me to Penguin.

I would also like to thank Vijesh from Penguin Chennai for buying into my book idea and introducing me to commissioning editor Anish Chandy, who gave the quickest response a first-time author can ever expect from a publisher. Within days, Anish was at my God's Own Office and my dream of being an author was sealed. Anish guided me in shaping the book and cleaned up many gaffes I made as a first-time author. Shatarupa Ghoshal and Udayan Mitra from Penguin for converting the manuscript to the final product and managing a very tight schedule. Vaarunya, my publicist from Penguin, for coming up with a great marketing plan for the book.

I would also like to acknowledge the various managers and mentors I had throughout my professional life, who went out of their way to help me fulfil my unorthodox dream—Sanjay Thapar, S. Sashidharan, Gopal Chandramowli, Partha Ragunathan, Sanjay Poonen, John Watton, Yvonne Puley, Peter Cummins, Punit Modhgil, Tarun Gulati, Rajan Anandan, Karan Bajwa and Bhaskar Pramanik.

Shaji Baby John for inviting me to Dubai in May 2013, to speak to a group of NRI professionals where I introduced the concept of God's Own Office for the first time. The overwhelming feedback I received in Dubai reassured the need for this book.

I salute the friendly and proactive customer service

staff of Jet Airways at Kochi airport and the caring staff at the various Taj hotels where I stayed, especially the Taj Lands End, for making my business travels a truly pleasant experience.

Finally, I would like acknowledge my siblings—four brothers and my only sister—for supporting my dreamy ideas at every stage of crisis in my life.